New York

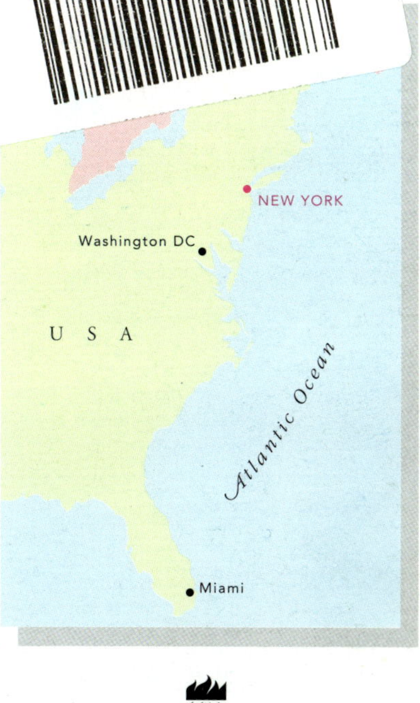

HarperCollins*Publishers*

YOUR COLLINS TRAVELLER

Your Collins Traveller Guide will help you find your way around your chosen destination quickly and simply. It is colour-coded for easy reference:

The blue section answers the question 'I would like to see or do something; where do I go and what do I see when I get there?' This section is arranged as an alphabetical list of topics. It is recommended that an up-to-date atlas or street plan is used in conjunction with the location maps in this section. Within each topic you will find:

- A selection of the best examples on offer.
- How to get there, costs and opening times for each entry.
- The outstanding features of each entry.
- A simplified map, with each entry plotted and the nearest landmark or transport access.

The red section is a lively and informative gazetteer. It offers:

- Essential facts about the main places and cultural items. What is La Bastille? Who was Michelangelo? Where is Delphi?

The gold section is full of practical and invaluable travel information. It offers:

- Everything you need to know to help you enjoy yourself and get the most out of your time away, from Accommodation through Baby-sitters, Car Hire, Food, Health, Money, Newspapers, Taxis and Telephones to Youth Hostels.

1993 PRICES	**Inexpensive**	**Moderate**	**Expensive**
Attractions			
Museums, etc	under $3	$3-7	over $7
Restaurants			
Meal, exc. wine	under $20	$20-35	over $35
Nightlife			
Clubs, discos, etc	See NIGHTLIFE 1-4		

Cross-references:

Type in small capitals – **CHURCHES** – tells you that more information on an item is available within the topic on churches.

A-Z after an item tells you that more information is available within the gazetteer. Simply look under the appropriate name.

A name in bold – **Holy Cathedral** – also tells you that more information on an item is available in the gazetteer – again simply look up the name.

CONTENTS

CONTENTS

PRACTICAL INFORMATION GAZETTEER

CONTENTS

PRACTICAL INFORMATION GAZETTEER continued

Bleecker Street

SHIBA
CAMERAS
COPIERS
VIDEO
MINOLTA
MARQUI
37
POLICE

INTRODUCTION

On a bus ride the length of Manhattan, you feel that you have traversed the best and worst that this planet has to offer: from the dangerous ghetto of Washington Heights, past beautiful Central Park, down the elite avenues of the Upper East Side, through the commercial cauldron of Midtown to the bohemian neighbourhoods of Downtown, and on to the modernist skyscrapers of the financial district. New York is a city full of contrasts in a confined space, where modernity and history, wealth and poverty, peace and freneticism lie cheek by jowl.

Standing among the most modern buildings in Midtown – or 'skyscraper national park', as Kurt Vonnegut puts it – you are overwhelmed by the awesome feats of modern design and engineering, and by their grace, beauty, sometimes their humour, sometimes their ugliness. And these same buildings share streets with lavishly ornamented 19thC blocks built on a human scale. At the same time, the historic brownstone buildings of Greenwich Village are but a short walk from the excesses of high-rise ambition around Wall St.

Such an architectural mix brings home the speed with which the city has evolved. In 1626 the Dutch West India Company created a small settlement on Manhattan called New Amsterdam, purchasing the island for $24 from Algonquin Indians. Ceded to the British in 1664 and renamed New York, it became part of the United States at the end of the War of American Independence in 1783. It was in the 19thC that the city established itself as the hub of US industry and commerce, a time when its population rose dramatically with an onslaught of immigrants, from Ireland and Germany initially, and later from Italy and Eastern Europe. By the end of the century, it was the world's largest city, with some 3 million inhabitants. The 20thC has taken the city on a roller coaster of a ride, with the birth of the skyscraper, the Crash in 1929 followed by the Great Depression, the arrival of the United Nations after World War II, and the World Trade Center and the growth of the financial district in the 1970s and '80s.

Despite their diverse origins, the people of New York could be said to have a common attitude. Like the immigrants who were processed through Ellis Island, people still come to the city to succeed. 'Lunch (or sleep, or holidays) is for wimps' is the philosophy, and yet New Yorkers

Brooklyn Bridge & Downtown Manhattan

seem to play just as hard as they work. You'll get the best out of locals if you're forthright: say what you want and how you want it, and don't fuss too much over pleases and thank yous (who's got time for pleasantries?). Don't appear shocked by the out of the ordinary, whether it's a man wandering in the street with a snake wrapped around his neck or a woman singing at the top of her voice on the subway: in New York anything goes, and shyness simply does not exist. You'll find yourself plagued by beggars though. Some may be enterprising, offering to declaim any passage from Shakespeare for a dollar. For an easy life, arm yourself with a pocketful of change each day.

In the daytime New York is as safe as any other modern city (and statistically safer than many others in the US). At night, by not flaunting your wealth or studying your street map at every corner, you'll lessen the chance of any nasty encounters. Don't treat as gospel *all* the danger stories residents tell you: New Yorkers revel in and therefore exaggerate the reputation of their city as a crime-infested metropolis.

The subway is a lot cleaner and better policed than it used to be. But take the bus – equally clean and efficient – if you're not in a hurry and want to see what's going on. As for taxis, drivers do not know where they are going, though they drive as if they do: a switchback, pothole-hitting, traffic-dodging ride from Downtown to Uptown is a quintessential and cheap New York experience. If you can (and if he understands English), tell your driver how to get to your final destination.

Chrysler Building

Statue of Liberty

However, you'll probably want to spend most of your time on foot. Each neighbourhood has its special time: Central Park on a weekend summer afternoon, the financial district on a weekday morning, East Village on a Fri. or Sat. night, Greenwich Village at Sun. lunchtime. Often there's so much going on that you feel your senses are going to burst through overuse, making sense of the Hemingway dictum, 'It's a town you come to for a short time.'

On a sunny day, put your feet up. It would be a crime to miss a view of the world's most famous skyline, so be sure to take to the water (or even splash out on a helicopter ride). The view is good enough to keep you enthralled for the full 3 hr of the Circle Line tour right round Manhattan. At the very least take the ferry to Staten Island, or the boat to the Statue of Liberty and Staten Island.

If you are only spending a short time in New York, other than taking a boat trip, you should stick to Manhattan. However, you should be

Woolworth Building

aware that Manhattan is not synonymous with New York City, but rather the most important of five boroughs. In addition, there are two urban boroughs – the Bronx and Brooklyn – and the suburban and rural boroughs of Queens and Staten Island.
It's not only on the streets that there's an exhausting amount to explore in Manhattan. An overwhelming choice of cuisine means that you could stay a month and eat different ethnic food every day. And eating out in New York can be very inexpensive (as well as exorbitant in some of the world's best restaurants). If you plan to walk all day you will need a big breakfast – the choice and the portions are huge. At lunchtime take 'a sandwich to go' – it will suffice for two average mortals. Tackle it in the street as the natives do.
You can 'shop till you drop', if you have the cash or the credit. This is the city that made shopping a career. Some shops may well be beyond your price range, but visit them anyway, for the experience and the name. You needn't buy anything – looking is still free – and you will be able to say, 'When I was in Bloomingdale's', or Macy's or Tiffany's. There are shops to suit every taste, age and bank account. You'll find discount stores where the prices of good-quality products are amazingly low. Give New York time and you will find exactly what you want at the right price.
When you've had enough of 5th Ave shops, you can feast your eyes on

some of the best art collections in the world. You will find an unrivalled range in the Metropolitan Museum (the Met), the Museum of Modern Art (MOMA), the Guggenheim, the Whitney and the beautiful Frick Collection (this gallery is a work of art in its own right).

After pounding the sidewalks you may want to sit back and be entertained. New York is the city where showbusiness was born. All tastes from the highest to the lowest are catered for and some of the best entertainment is free. No summer visitor with an afternoon and evening to spare (except Mon.) should miss Shakespeare in the Park. The Theater District, around Broadway and 42nd St, and its 'suburbs', Off-Broadway and Off-Off-Broadway, will add to your experience without necessarily costing you a week's wages, although you could pay this if you want to see the latest Broadway hit musical. If the straight theatre is too straight for you, the bars, cabarets and music clubs will have you dancing, singing and laughing – perhaps all three at once! Should something more refined be required, the Lincoln Center and Carnegie Hall will offer you a full choice.

Accommodation can make a real hole in your budget in New York. If possible, stay with friends (or friends of friends if necessary). Otherwise you may want to consider a package deal. Bed and breakfast American-style, where you may be sleeping on a sofa in your host's sitting-room, is still pricey for what you get, but offers a good way of meeting locals and being able to stay in areas devoid of hotels like Greenwich Village.

Everyone has their favourite season for being in the city. Some contend that as a city of extremes it's best experienced in the extreme temperatures of summer or winter when visitors can join forces with inhabitants in a fight against the heat and humidity or icy cold. Others say the city is most beautiful in the autumn. However, you'll experience most classic images at any time of the year, whether it's steam billowing out of a manhole cover, a subway rattling under the sidewalk, or a cockroach scurrying across the bedroom floor (don't be too alarmed – they're very common). Whenever you visit New York, if you're bored it's your own fault. This has got to be the most exhilarating city in the world. 'Enjoy!', everyone barks at you – it isn't difficult.

Central Park
Central Park West
COLUMBUS
Queensboro Br.
West 57th St
East 57th St
QUEENS
P.J. CLARKE'S
Broadway
BLUE BAR
AT THE
ALGONQUIN
West 42nd St
East 42nd St
West 34th St
East 34th St
Twelfth Avenue
Eighth Avenue
Fifth Avenue
First Avenue
East River
PETE'S
TAVERN
West 14th St
East 14th St
McSORLEY'S
OLD ALE
HOUSE
WHITE HORSE
TAVERN
Hudson River
PECULIER
PUB
LION'S
HEAD
East Houston St
MANHATTAN
BREWING
COMPANY
Canal St
West St
HOBOKEN
Broadway
Brooklyn Br.
BROOKLYN

BLUE BAR AT THE ALGONQUIN 59 W 44th St.
See **Opening Times**. B, D, F to 42nd St, 7 to 5th Ave. Bus M5-M7.
Dim, romantic and cosy, attracting indiscreet celebrities.

COLUMBUS 201 Columbus Ave at 69th St. See **Opening Times**.
B, C, 1-3 to 72nd St; 1 to Lincoln Center. Bus M7, M11.
Another good place for celebrity-spotting.

LION'S HEAD 59 Christopher St, off Sheridan Sq. See **Opening Times**. 1 to Christopher St/Sheridan Sq. Bus M5, M6, M8, M10.
NYC's writers' pub. The place to come if you've any literary pretensions.

MANHATTAN BREWING COMPANY 40 Thompson St at Watts St. See **Opening Times**. A, C, E to Canal St. Bus M5, M6, M10, M21. *Hard-to-find beers from around the US; some brewed on premises.*

McSORLEY'S OLD ALE HOUSE 15 E 7th St. See **Opening Times**. 6 to Astor Pl. Bus M8, M15, M101, M102.
One of the city's oldest pubs (women used to be barred!). Good beer.

PECULIER PUB 145 Bleecker St, between Thompson St and La Guardia. See **Opening Times**. A-F to Washington Sq. Bus M1, M5, M6, M21. *A selection of over 200 beers from all over the world.*

PETE'S TAVERN 129 E 18th St at Irving Pl. See **Opening Times**.
L, N, R, 4-6 to Union Sq. Bus M101, M102.
The oldest bar in NYC. An air of simplicity and quiet prevails.

P.J. CLARKE'S 915 3rd Ave at 55th St. See **Opening Times**.
E, F to Lexington Ave. Bus M1-M4, M32, M88, M101, M102.
A classic, old, Irish saloon bar. Good at any time, but best late at night.

WHITE HORSE TAVERN 567 Hudson St at W 11th St. See **Opening Times**. A, C, E to 14th St; 1 to Christopher St/Sheridan Sq. Bus M10, M11, M14. *Dylan Thomas had his last drink here. Good juke-box. Street café in summer.*

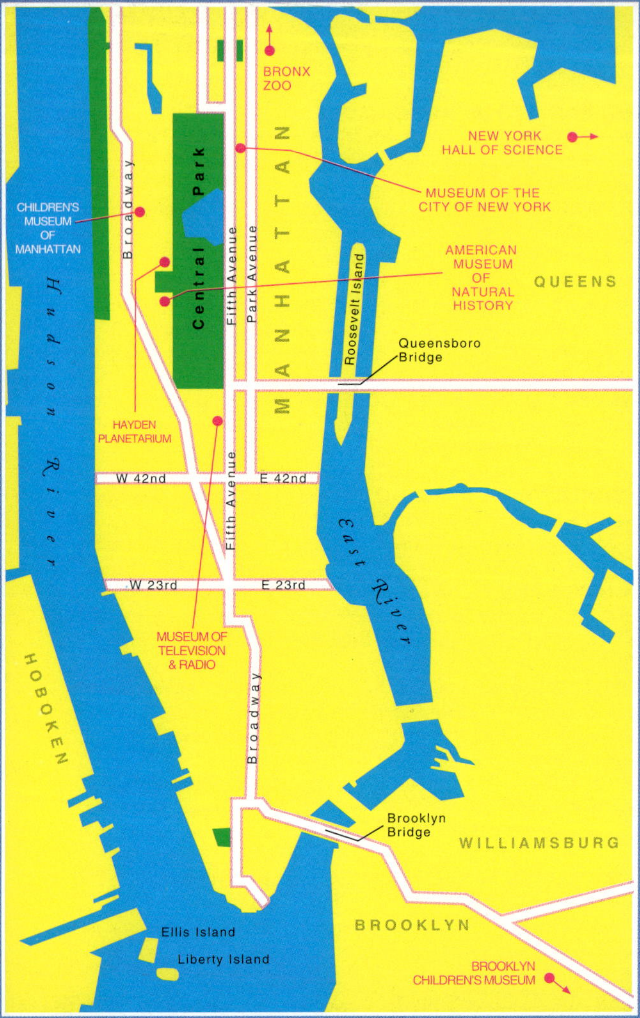
BRONX ZOO
NEW YORK HALL OF SCIENCE
MUSEUM OF THE CITY OF NEW YORK
CHILDREN'S MUSEUM OF MANHATTAN
Broadway
Central Park
Fifth Avenue
Park Avenue
MANHATTAN
AMERICAN MUSEUM OF NATURAL HISTORY
QUEENS
Roosevelt Island
Queensboro Bridge
Hudson River
HAYDEN PLANETARIUM
W 42nd
E 42nd
East River
W 23rd
E 23rd
MUSEUM OF TELEVISION & RADIO
HOBOKEN
Brooklyn Bridge
WILLIAMSBURG
BROOKLYN
Ellis Island
Liberty Island
BROOKLYN CHILDREN'S MUSEUM

AMERICAN MUSEUM OF NATURAL HISTORY Central Park West at 79th St. ▪ 1000-1745 Sun.-Thu., 1000-2045 Fri. & Sat. S 1, 9 to 79th St; B, C to 81st St. Bus M7, M10, M11. ● Donation (suggest Moderate). *Famous for its extensive dinosaur bones collection. See* **A-Z**.

BRONX ZOO Bronx River Parkway at Fordham Rd. ▪ 1000-1700 Mon.-Fri., 1000-1730 Sat. & Sun. S 2, 5 to E 180th St. ● Moderate. Donation Wed. *World's largest – educational and entertaining. See* **A-Z**.

BROOKLYN CHILDREN'S MUSEUM 145 Brooklyn Ave. ▪ 1200-1700 Sat.-Mon., 1400-1700 Wed.-Fri. S 2-4 to Eastern Parkway/Brooklyn Museum. ● Donation (suggest Moderate). *World's first children's museum, with opportunities to join in as well as to look.*

CHILDREN'S MUSEUM OF MANHATTAN 212 W 83rd St. ▪ 1100-1700 Tue.-Fri., 1200-1700 Sat. S 1, 9 to 86th St; B, C to 81st St. Bus M7, M11, M86, M104. ● Moderate.
Exciting hands-on educational displays and activities.

HAYDEN PLANETARIUM Central Park West at 81st St. ▪ 1230-1700 Mon.-Fri., 1000-1745 Sat., 1200-1745 Sun. S B, C to 81st St; 1, 9 to 79th St. Bus M7, M10, M11. ● Moderate. *Sky shows and laser spectaculars accompanied by rock music. See* **A-Z**.

MUSEUM OF TELEVISION & RADIO 25 W 52nd St. ▪ 1200-1800 Tue.-Sun. (until 2000 Thu.). S B, D, F to Rockefeller Center. Bus M1-M5, M27, M50. ● Moderate. *Watch your favourite TV shows from the archives (go early for the best choice).*

MUSEUM OF THE CITY OF NEW YORK 5th Ave at 103rd St. ▪ 1000-1700 Wed.-Sat., 1300-1700 Sun. & hols. S 6 to 103rd St. Bus M1-M4. ● Moderate. *Toy gallery, old fire engines, etc. See* **MUSEUMS 2**.

NEW YORK HALL OF SCIENCE 47-01 111th St, Queens. ▪ 1000-1700. S 7 to 111th St. ● Moderate. *Hands-on learning and fun, including why Catseyes glow in the dark and what electricity is.*

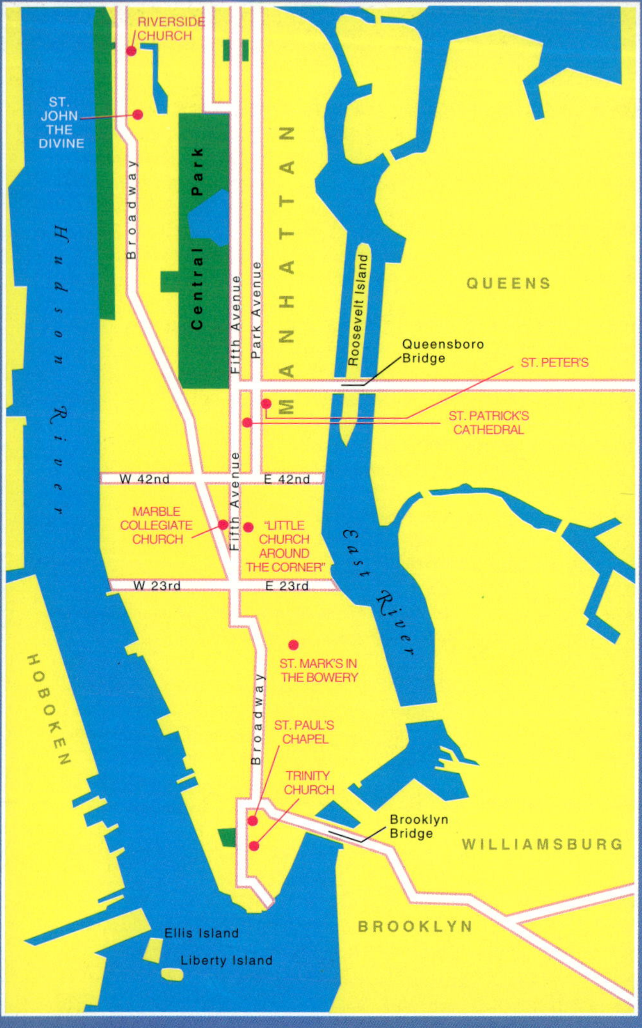
RIVERSIDE CHURCH
ST. JOHN THE DIVINE
Broadway
Central Park
Fifth Avenue
Park Avenue
MANHATTAN
Hudson River
Roosevelt Island
QUEENS
Queensboro Bridge
ST. PETER'S
ST. PATRICK'S CATHEDRAL
W 42nd
E 42nd
MARBLE COLLEGIATE CHURCH
"LITTLE CHURCH AROUND THE CORNER"
East River
W 23rd
E 23rd
HOBOKEN
ST. MARK'S IN THE BOWERY
ST. PAUL'S CHAPEL
TRINITY CHURCH
Brooklyn Bridge
WILLIAMSBURG
BROOKLYN
Ellis Island
Liberty Island

'LITTLE CHURCH AROUND THE CORNER' 29th St east of 5th Ave. S N, R to 28th St/Broadway. Bus M2, M3, M5, M32.
A favourite with theatre people. The church has a certain country-cottage appeal which makes it popular for weddings. See **A-Z**.

MARBLE COLLEGIATE CHURCH 5th Ave at 29th St.
S N, R to 28th St/Broadway. Bus M2, M3, M5, M32.
The oldest Protestant church in the USA (founded in 1628). See **A-Z**.

RIVERSIDE CHURCH 122nd St at Riverside Drive.
S 1, 9 to 116th St. Bus M4, M5, M104.
Climb the tower for good views of the city. See **A-Z**.

ST. JOHN THE DIVINE 112th St at Amsterdam Ave.
S B, C, 1, 9 to Cathedral Parkway/110th St. Bus M4, M11.
The largest Gothic-style cathedral in the world (still unfinished). See **A-Z**.

ST. MARK'S IN THE BOWERY 2nd Ave at 10th St.
S N, R, 4-6 to 14th St/Union Sq. Bus M15.
This busy community church hosts readings and concerts. See **A-Z**.

ST. PATRICK'S CATHEDRAL 5th Ave at 50th St.
S B, D, F to Rockefeller Center. Bus M1-M5, M27.
Large Gothic-style cathedral with a splendid interior. See **A-Z**.

ST. PAUL'S CHAPEL Broadway at Fulton St.
S A, C, J, M, Z, 2-5 to Fulton St/Broadway. Bus M1, M6.
The oldest church in Manhattan, dating from 1766. See **A-Z**.

ST. PETER'S Lexington Ave at 54th St.
S E, F to Lexington Ave/53rd St. Bus M98, M101, M102.
Lutheran church which has become part of the Citicorp Center (see **A-Z***).*

TRINITY CHURCH Broadway at Wall St.
S 4, 5 to Wall St/Broadway. Bus M1, M6.
Small church with its own museum. See **A-Z**.

HARLEM
MANHATTAN
Central Park
Broadway
UPPER WEST SIDE
UPPER EAST SIDE
QUEENS
Fifth Avenue
Park Avenue
Roosevelt Island
Queensboro Bridge
Hudson River
THEATER DISTRICT
W 42nd
E 42nd
W 23rd
E 23rd
East River
GREENWICH VILLAGE
EAST VILLAGE
SOHO
LITTLE ITALY
TRIBECA
CHINATOWN
HOBOKEN
Brooklyn Bridge
WILLIAMSBURG
BROOKLYN
Ellis Island
Liberty Island

CHINATOWN/LITTLE ITALY Canal St to East Broadway, Bowery St to Canal St/Canal St to Kenmore St, Centre St to Bowery St. S J, M, N, R, Z, 6 to Canal St; B, D, Q to Grand St. Bus M1, M9, M15, M22, M101, M102.
Two areas which have almost merged geographically. There are hundreds of Chinese and Italian restaurants and shops. See **A-Z**.

EAST VILLAGE Broadway to Ave D, Houston St to 14th St. S F to 2nd Ave. Bus M15, M101, M102.
Slightly seedy home of punks, artists and East Europeans. See **A-Z**.

GREENWICH VILLAGE 14th St to Houston St, west of Broadway to the Hudson River. S A-F to W 4th St; 1, 9 to Christopher St. Bus M1, M5, M6, M10. *Bars, restaurants and shops. Great for street life. See* **A-Z**.

HARLEM 96th St to 168th St, the Hudson River to the Harlem River. S A-D, 1-6, 9 to 125th St. Bus M1, M2, M7, M10, M102.
Attractions include Hamilton Grange (see **A-Z***), Grant's Tomb (see* **A-Z***), Cloisters (see* **A-Z***) and Audubon Terrace (see* **A-Z***). See* **A-Z**.

SOHO/TRIBECA Houston St to Chambers St, Broadway to the Hudson River. S A, C, E, 1, 9 to Canal St; C, E, 6 to Spring St. Bus M1, M5, M6, M10. *Admire the cast-iron buildings (see* **A-Z***) and historic landmarks. See* **A-Z**.

THEATER DISTRICT 42nd St to 59th St, 7th Ave to the Hudson River. S A, C, E, N, R, 1-3, 7, 9 to 42nd St. Bus M5-M7, M10, M104.
Busy 24 hr a day. Most Broadway shows are staged here. See **Theatre**.

UPPER EAST SIDE 59th St to 96th St, 5th Ave to the East River. S 6 to 77th St. Bus M1-M4, M15, M101, M102.
Famous people reside in this patrician district. Lively nightlife.

UPPER WEST SIDE Central Park West to the Hudson River, 59th St to 90th St. S 1, 9 to 79th St. Bus M5, M7, M10, M11, M104.
Up-market residential area with boutiques, cafés and bars.

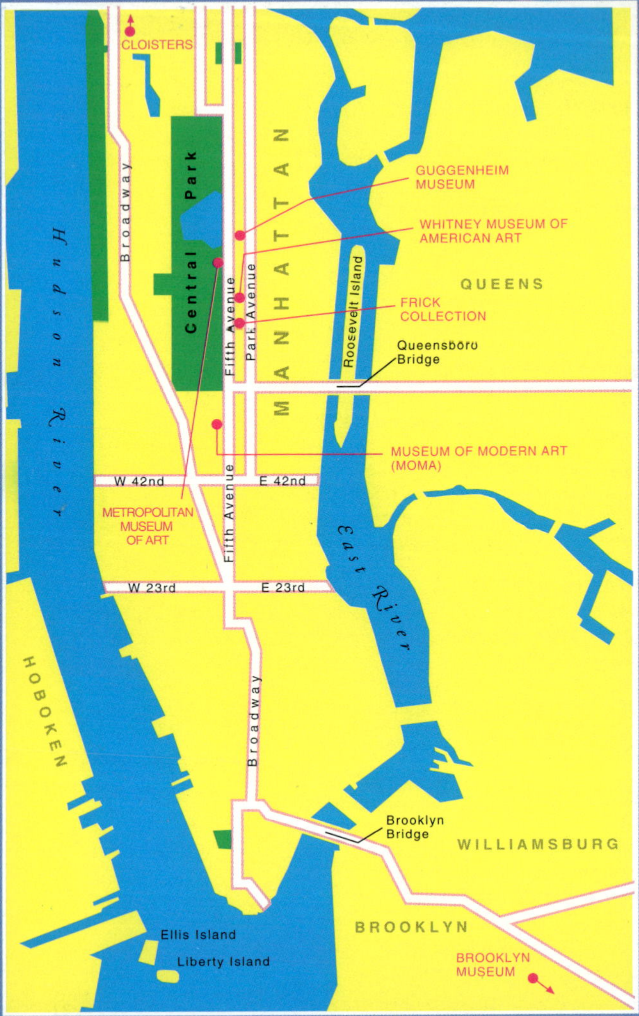
CLOISTERS
Broadway
Central Park
Hudson River
MANHATTAN
GUGGENHEIM MUSEUM
WHITNEY MUSEUM OF AMERICAN ART
Fifth Avenue
Park Avenue
Roosevelt Island
QUEENS
FRICK COLLECTION
Queensboro Bridge
MUSEUM OF MODERN ART (MOMA)
W 42nd
E 42nd
METROPOLITAN MUSEUM OF ART
East River
W 23rd
E 23rd
HOBOKEN
Brooklyn Bridge
WILLIAMSBURG
BROOKLYN
Ellis Island
Liberty Island
BROOKLYN MUSEUM

BROOKLYN MUSEUM 200 Eastern Parkway, Brooklyn. 1000-1700 Wed.-Mon. S 2-4 to Eastern Parkway/Brooklyn Museum. Moderate. *One of America's leading museums of art, with everything from Oriental, African, Asian and native American art to photographs, drawings and prints. See* **A-Z**.

FRICK COLLECTION 1 E 70th St. 1000-1800 Tue.-Sat., 1300-1800 Sun. Closed hols. S 6 to 68th St/Hunter College/Lexington Ave. Bus M1-M4. Inexpensive. Under 10s not admitted. *If you choose only one museum to visit, the Frick Collection should be it. See* **A-Z**.

GUGGENHEIM MUSEUM 5th Ave at 89th St. 1000-2000 Fri.-Wed. S 4-6 to 86th St. Bus M1-M4. Moderate. Voluntary donation after 1700 Tue. *Modern art in an extravagant building by Frank Lloyd Wright. See* **A-Z**.

METROPOLITAN MUSEUM OF ART 5th Ave at 82nd St. 0930-1715 Tue.-Thu. & Sun., 0930-2045 Fri. & Sat. S 4-6 to 86th St. Bus M1-M4. Moderate (includes admission to Cloisters – see below). *Remarkable art collection. Free daily highlights tour. See* **A-Z**.

CLOISTERS Fort Tryon Park. 0930-1715 Tue.-Sun. S A to 190th St. Bus M4. Moderate (includes admission to Metropolitan Museum of Art – see above). *Houses the Metropolitan's vast collection of medieval art. See* **A-Z**.

MUSEUM OF MODERN ART (MOMA) 11 W 53rd St. 1100-1800 Fri.-Tue., 1100-2100 Thu. S E, F to 53rd St/5th Ave; B, C, F, S to Rockefeller Center. Bus M1-M5. Moderate. Voluntary donation Thu. *The favourite meeting place of wealthy New Yorkers. Pleasing setting. See* **A-Z**.

WHITNEY MUSEUM OF AMERICAN ART 945 Madison Ave at 75th St. 1100-1800 Tue., Wed. & Fri.-Sun., 1300-2000 Thu. S 6 to 77th St. Bus M1-M4, M30, M72. Moderate.
Houses a comprehensive collection of American art. See **A-Z**.

MUSEUM OF THE AMERICAN INDIAN
MUSEUM OF THE CITY OF NEW YORK
Broadway
Central Park
Fifth Avenue
Park Avenue
MANHATTAN
QUEENS
JEWISH MUSEUM
COOPER-HEWITT MUSEUM
NATIONAL ACADEMY OF DESIGN
AMERICAN MUSEUM OF THE MOVING IMAGE
Roosevelt Island
Queensboro Bridge
Hudson River
W 42nd
E 42nd
PIERPONT MORGAN LIBRARY
East River
W 23rd
E 23rd
HOBOKEN
Broadway
Brooklyn Bridge
WILLIAMSBURG
BROOKLYN
Ellis Island
Liberty Island

AMERICAN MUSEUM OF THE MOVING IMAGE 36th St at 35th Ave, Astoria, Queens. ▪ 1200-1600 Tue.-Fri., 1200-1800 Sat. & Sun. S R to Steinway St. ● Moderate.
Memorabilia and high-tech exhibits tracing the history of film.

COOPER-HEWITT MUSEUM 2 E 91st St. ▪ 1000-2100 Tue., 1000-1700 Wed.-Sat., 1200-1700 Sun. S 4-6 to 86th St. Bus M1-M4, M19. ● Inexpensive.
A changing programme of exhibitions on the decorative arts. See **A-Z**.

JEWISH MUSEUM 5th Ave at 92nd St. ▪ 1200-1700 Mon., Wed. & Thu., 1200-2000 Tue., 1100-1800 Sun. S 6 to 96th St. Bus M1-M4, M19. ● Inexpensive.
A large collection of religious objects, cultural artefacts, and modern Jewish art, including Holocaust *by the sculptor George Segal.*

PIERPONT MORGAN LIBRARY 29 E 36th St at Madison Ave. ▪ 1030-1700 Tue.-Sat., 1300-1700 Sun. Closed Aug. & Sun. in July. S 6 to 33rd St. Bus M1-M3, M32. ● Moderate.
Precious medieval manuscripts, rare books and works of art, including Rembrandt prints. See **A-Z**.

MUSEUM OF THE AMERICAN INDIAN Broadway at 155th St. ▪ 1000-1700 Tue.-Sat., 1300-1700 Sun. S 1 to 157th St. Bus M4, M5. ● Inexpensive.
Marvellous representation of Indian culture. Well worth visiting.

MUSEUM OF THE CITY OF NEW YORK 5th Ave at 103rd St. ▪ 1000-1700 Wed.-Sat., 1300-1700 Sun. & hols. S 6 to 103rd St. Bus M1-M4. ● Moderate.
The Big Apple Show *is a good introduction to NY's history. See* **CHILDREN**.

NATIONAL ACADEMY OF DESIGN 5th Ave at 89th St. ▪ 1200-1700 Wed.-Sun. (until 2000 Fri.). S 4-6 to 86th St. Bus M1-M4. ● Moderate. Free after 1700 Fri.
19th-20thC American portraiture, painting, sculpture, photography, etc.

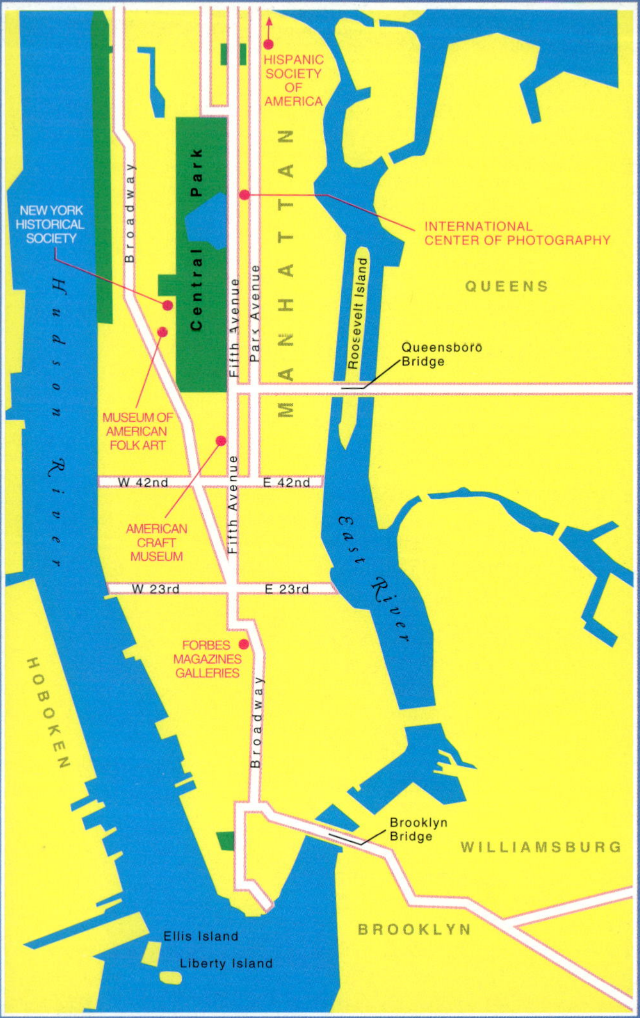

HISPANIC SOCIETY OF AMERICA
NEW YORK HISTORICAL SOCIETY
Broadway
Central Park
Fifth Avenue
Park Avenue
MANHATTAN
INTERNATIONAL CENTER OF PHOTOGRAPHY
Roosevelt Island
QUEENS
Queensboro Bridge
Hudson River
MUSEUM OF AMERICAN FOLK ART
W 42nd
E 42nd
AMERICAN CRAFT MUSEUM
East River
W 23rd
E 23rd
FORBES MAGAZINES GALLERIES
HOBOKEN
Brooklyn Bridge
WILLIAMSBURG
BROOKLYN
Ellis Island
Liberty Island

AMERICAN CRAFT MUSEUM 40 W 53rd St at 5th Ave. ■ 1000-2000 Tue., 1000-1700 Wed.-Sun. S B, D, F to Rockefeller Center. Bus M1-M4, M27, M32. ● Moderate. Free after 1700 Tue.
Permanent collection of the best of 20thC American crafts, sponsored by the American Craft Council, plus interesting temporary exhibits.

FORBES MAGAZINES GALLERIES 62 5th Ave at 12th St. ■ 1000-1600 Tue., Wed., Fri. & Sat. S L, N, R, 4-6 to Union Sq. Bus M1-M3, M5. ● Free.
Exhibits include toy boats and soldiers, and the largest collection of Fabergé Easter eggs in the world.

HISPANIC SOCIETY OF AMERICA Broadway and 155th St. ■ 1000-1630 Tue.-Sat., 1300-1600 Sun. S 1 to Broadway/157th St. Bus M4, M5. ● Free.
In Audubon Terrace (see **A-Z***), this is a wonderful display of Spanish art and artefacts, including paintings by El Greco, Velázquez and Goya.*

INTERNATIONAL CENTER OF PHOTOGRAPHY 1130 5th Ave. ■ 1100-1800 Wed.-Sun., 1100-2000 Tue. S 6 to Lexington Ave/96th St. Bus M1-M4, M19. ● Moderate. Free after 1700 Tue.
Permanent display of works by Cartier-Bresson, Adams and Kertesz in this elegant, early-20thC town house. Good temporary exhibitions.

MUSEUM OF AMERICAN FOLK ART 2 Lincoln Sq. (Columbus Ave, between W 65th St and W 66th St). ■ 1130-1930. S 1, 9 to 66th St. Bus M5-M7. ● Inexpensive.
Early American hand-crafted quilts, toys, signs, decoys, weather vanes, etc. Also changing displays, plus craft demonstrations.

NEW YORK HISTORICAL SOCIETY Central Park West at 77th St. ■ 1100-1700 Tue., Wed., Fri. & Sun., 1100-2000 Thu. S B, C to 81st St. ● Moderate. Donation Tue.
The city's oldest museum was founded in 1804 and houses American folk art, Colonial artefacts, antique toys, old prints and maps, and coaches. See **A-Z**.

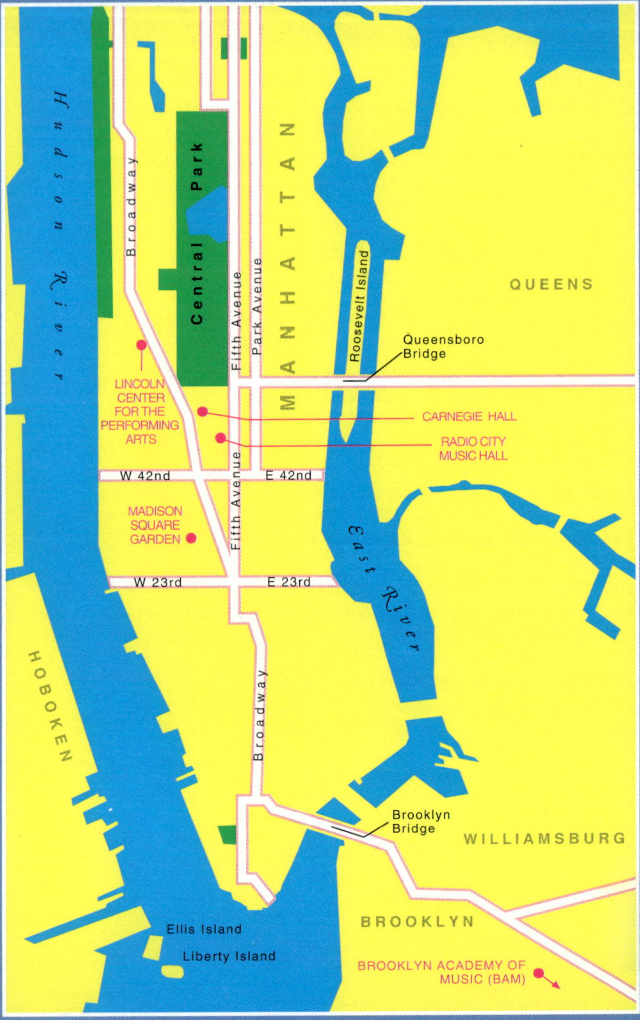
Hudson River
Broadway
Central Park
Fifth Avenue
Park Avenue
MANHATTAN
Roosevelt Island
QUEENS
Queensboro Bridge
LINCOLN CENTER FOR THE PERFORMING ARTS
CARNEGIE HALL
RADIO CITY MUSIC HALL
W 42nd
E 42nd
MADISON SQUARE GARDEN
East River
W 23rd
E 23rd
HOBOKEN
Brooklyn Bridge
WILLIAMSBURG
BROOKLYN
Ellis Island
Liberty Island
BROOKLYN ACADEMY OF MUSIC (BAM)

BROOKLYN ACADEMY OF MUSIC (BAM)
30 Lafayette Ave, tel: 718-6364100. S D, Q, 2-5 to Atlantic Ave.
The oldest performing arts academy in the US. Legendary figures such as Isadora Duncan and Gertrude Stein have appeared here. See **A-Z**.

CARNEGIE HALL
154 W 57th St, tel: 2477800. S 1, 9, A, D to Columbus Circle; N, R to 57th St; B, D, E to 7th Ave; Q to 57th St. Bus M5-M7.
The acoustics in this world-famous concert hall are superb. All the greats have played here, from Mahler to Sinatra. See **A-Z**.

LINCOLN CENTER FOR THE PERFORMING ARTS
Broadway at 64th St. S 1, 9 to Lincoln Center. Bus M5, M7, M10, M11, M66, M104.
The Lincoln Center was opened by John D. Rockefeller (see **A-Z***), one of its main benefactors, in the 1960s. The complex incorporates the following theatres and concert halls:* **Avery Fisher Hall**, *tel: 8755030, a concert hall seating 2700, which is the home of the New York Philharmonic, conducted by Kurt Masur, and hosts the New York Film Festival every Sep.;* **Metropolitan Opera House (The Met)**, *tel: 3626000, a huge theatre with Chagall murals in the lobby, where the Metropolitan Opera Company performs Sep.-April and the American Ballet Theater May & June;* **New York State Theater**, *tel: 8705570, seating nearly 3000 and putting on productions by New York City Ballet; and* **Alice Tully Hall**, *tel: 3621911, designed for chamber music and recitals.*

MADISON SQUARE GARDEN
7th Ave at 33rd St, tel: 465-MSGI. S A, C, E, 1-3, 9 to Penn Station. Bus M4, M10, M16.
Hosts superstars like Michael Jackson and Bruce Springsteen. See **A-Z**.

RADIO CITY MUSIC HALL
50th St and 6th Ave, tel: 2474777. S B, D, F, Q to Rockefeller Center. Bus M5-M7, M27, M32, M50.
A huge indoor music hall. Pop and rock concerts by groups ranging from The Grateful Dead to The Temptations. See **Rockefeller Center**.

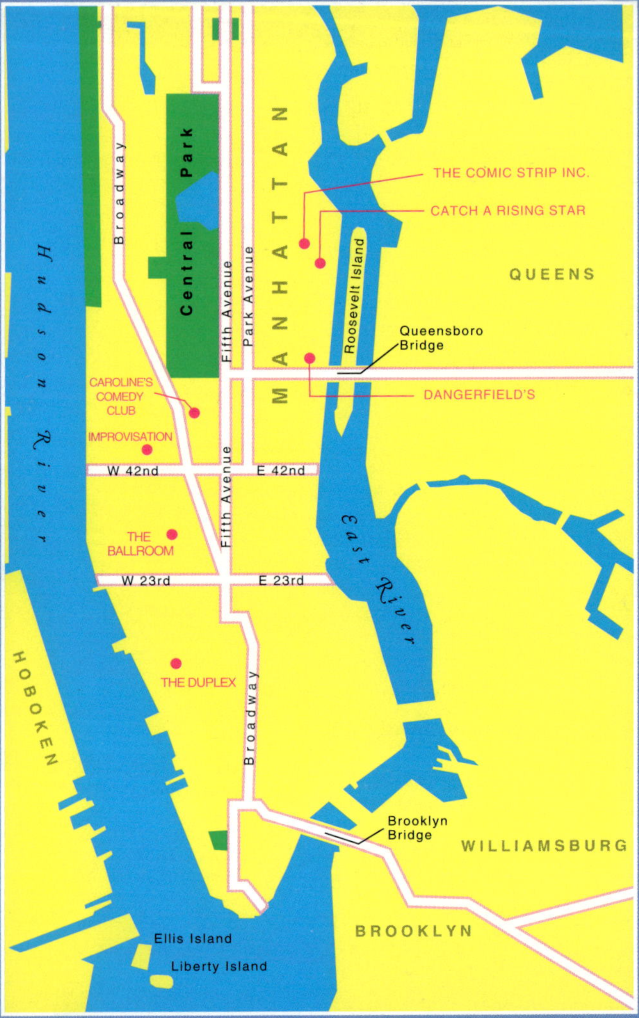
Broadway
Central Park
MANHATTAN
Fifth Avenue
Park Avenue
THE COMIC STRIP INC.
CATCH A RISING STAR
Roosevelt Island
QUEENS
Queensboro Bridge
DANGERFIELD'S
Hudson River
CAROLINE'S COMEDY CLUB
IMPROVISATION
W 42nd
E 42nd
Fifth Avenue
East River
THE BALLROOM
W 23rd
E 23rd
HOBOKEN
THE DUPLEX
Broadway
Brooklyn Bridge
WILLIAMSBURG
BROOKLYN
Ellis Island
Liberty Island

Comedy

Admission charges vary ($7-12 Sun.-Thu., $12 upwards Fri. & Sat.). Most clubs have a two-drink, or set-price drinks and food, minimum.

CAROLINE'S COMEDY CLUB 1626 Broadway, between 49th St and 50th St, tel: 7574100. 2000 Tue.-Thu. & Sun., 2000 & 2230 Fri. & Sat. S 1, 9 to 50th St. Bus M10, M27, M104. *A slick venue for some of New York's biggest stand-ups.*

CATCH A RISING STAR 1487 1st Ave at 77th St, tel: 7941906. 2100 Sun.-Thu., 2030 & 2300 Fri., 1930 Sat. (1st show). S 6 to 77th St/Lexington Ave. Bus M15. *A showcase for new talent, with the occasional return of an established star.*

THE COMIC STRIP INC. 1568 2nd Ave between 81st St and 82nd St, tel: 8619386. 2100 Mon.-Thu., 2030 & 2245 Fri., 2000 Sat. (1st show), 2030 Sun. S 4-6 to 86th St. Bus M15. *Many of the greats were 'discovered' here, including Eddie Murphy.*

DANGERFIELD'S 1118 1st Ave between E 61st St and E 62nd St, tel: 5931650. 2045 Sun.-Thu., 2100 & 2300 Fri., 2000, 2230 & 0030 Sat. S 4-6 59th St/Lexington Ave. Bus M15, M31. *This club was founded by the famous comedian Rodney Dangerfield.*

THE DUPLEX 61 Christopher St at 7th Ave South, tel: 2555438. 2000 & 2200 Sun.-Thu., 2200 & 2400 Fri. & Sat. S 1, 9 to Christopher St/Sheridan Sq. Bus M5, M6, M10, M13. *Woody Allen, Joan Rivers and Rodney Dangerfield all started out in cabaret here.*

IMPROVISATION 358 W 44th St at 9th Ave, tel: 7658268. 2100 Sun.-Thu., 2115 & 2345 Fri., 2030 & 2315 Sat. S A, C, E to 42nd St/8th Ave. Bus M5-M7, M10, M27, M42. *Many of the greats return here to pay tribute and try out new material.*

THE BALLROOM 253 28th St, between 7th Ave and 8th Ave, tel: 2443005. 2100 & 2300 Tue.-Sun. S 1, 9 to 28th St. Bus M10. *Popular singers appear regularly. Sample the Spanish* tapas *(snacks).*

Central Park
Central Park West
COPACABANA
Queensboro Br.
West 57th St
East 57th St
QUEENS
ROSELAND
USA
Broadway
West 42nd St
East 42nd St
West 34th St
East 34th St
East River
Twelfth Avenue
SOUND FACTORY
Eighth Avenue
LIMELIGHT
Fifth Avenue
First Avenue
West 14th St
East 14th St
Hudson River
East Houston St
SOB'S
Canal St
West St
HOBOKEN
Broadway
Brooklyn Br.
BROOKLYN

Dance Clubs

Admission charges vary nightly. $15-20 is about average. Some may charge less but have a two-drink minimum.

COPACABANA 10 E 60th St, near 5th Ave, tel: 7556010.
From 2200. S N, R to 60th St/5th Ave. Bus M1-M4.
Latin American and disco music. It's changed since Barry Manilow described it in song, but it still packs 'em in.

LIMELIGHT 47 W 20th St at 6th Ave, tel: 8077850.
2200-0400. S F to 23rd St. Bus M2, M3, M5-M7.
Stroboscopes and house music in a cavernous church building. Dancers strut in metal cages.

ROSELAND 239 W 52nd St, between 7th Ave and 8th Ave, tel: 2470200. 1430-0500 Thu.-Sun. S 1, 9 to 50th St/Broadway. Bus M6, M7, M10, M104.
Ballroom dancing to big bands in the afternoons and evenings, and a disco late at night in this legendary establishment opened in 1919. Restaurant and bar.

SOB'S 204 Varick St at W Houston St, tel: 2434940.
Telephone for opening times. S 1, 9 to Houston St/Varick St. Bus M10, M21.
Dance all night to the rhythms of Latin America, disco, jazz and salsa performed by live bands.

SOUND FACTORY 542 W 27th St at 10th Ave, tel: 6430728.
0100-1200. S C, E to 23rd St/8th Ave.
The place to head for when all the other clubs are beginning to close. Predominantly gay.

USA 218 W 47th St between Broadway and 8th Ave, tel: 8696103.
2200-0400 Wed.-Sun. S 1, 9 to 50th St; N, R to 49th St. Bus M10, M27, M104.
New, massive, state-of-the-art club with pop art, fairground slide and kinky paraphernalia.

Central Park
Central Park West
Queensboro Br.
West 57th St
East 57th St
QUEENS
MICHAEL'S PUB
RED BLAZER TOO
Broadway
West 42nd St
East 42nd St
West 34th St
East 34th St
East River
Twelfth Avenue
Eighth Avenue
Fifth Avenue
First Avenue
FAT TUESDAY'S
West 14th St
East 14th St
VILLAGE VANGUARD
Hudson River
BLUE NOTE
VILLAGE GATE
East Houston St
Canal St
West St
HOBOKEN
Broadway
Brooklyn Br.
BROOKLYN

Admission charges vary nightly. Inexpensive is under $15, Moderate $15-30 and Expensive over $30.

BLUE NOTE 131 W 3rd St, tel: 4758592. 2100 & 2330 daily (plus 0100 Fri. & Sat.). A-F to W 4th St/Washington Sq. Bus M5, M6, M10. Expensive. Cover charge varies.
The *place to hear jazz greats and legends in the making. Jam here for free after 0200.*

FAT TUESDAY'S 190 3rd Ave at 17th St, tel: 5337900. 2000 & 2200 daily (plus 2400 Fri. & Sat.). L, N, R, 4-6 to Union Sq./14th St. Bus M2, M7, M101, M102. Moderate.
Popular basement jazz club featuring well-known musicians. Bar and restaurant at ground level.

MICHAEL'S PUB 211 E 55th St, between 3rd Ave and 2nd Ave, tel: 7582272. 2100 & 2300 Mon.-Sat. E, F to Lexington Ave/53rd St. Bus M1-M5, M27, M32, M50. Moderate-Expensive.
Nostalgic jazz. Woody Allen plays clarinet on Mon. when he's in town.

RED BLAZER TOO 349 W 46th St, between 8th Ave and 9th Ave, tel: 2623112. 2100-0100. A, C, E to 42nd St. Bus M10, M27, M104. Inexpensive.
Jazz spot featuring big bands and great Dixieland. Dinner and dancing.

VILLAGE GATE Corner of Bleecker St and Thompson St, tel: 4755120. 1800-0200. A-F to W 4th St/Washington Sq. Bus M1, M5, M6. Inexpensive. Cover charge varies. *This club at the heart of the New York jazz scene is more like a hall. There are a bar and café upstairs.*

VILLAGE VANGUARD 178 7th Ave South at Perry St and Waverley Pl., tel: 2554037. 2130, 2330 & 0100. 1, 9 to Christopher St/Sheridan Sq. Bus M10. Moderate.
All the greats have played, and still come to play, at this jazz institution. No food served.

Central Park West
Central Park
Queensboro Br.
West 57th St
East 57th St
QUEENS
THE RITZ
Broadway
West 42nd St
East 42nd St
West 34th St
East 34th St
East River
Twelfth Avenue
TRAMPS
EAGLE TAVERN
Eighth Avenue
Fifth Avenue
First Avenue
West 14th St
East 14th St
Hudson River
BOTTOM LINE
SPEAKEASY
CBGB
THE BITTER END
East Houston St
Canal St
West St
HOBOKEN
Broadway
Brooklyn Br.
BROOKLYN

Rock, Folk & Blues

Inexpensive admission charges are under $10, Moderate $10-20 and Expensive over $20.

THE BITTER END 149 Bleecker St, tel: 6737030. Opens 1700. Show starts 2130. S A-F to W 4th St/Washington Sq. Bus M1-M3, M5, M6, M8. Inexpensive. *A showcase for some of the greatest when they started out. Features rock and other styles of music.*

BOTTOM LINE 15 W 4th St at Mercer St, tel: 2286300. Opens 1900. Shows at 2000 & 2300. S A-F to W 4th St/Washington Sq. Bus M1, M5, M6, M101, M102. Moderate-Expensive. *Big-name bands.*

CBGB 315 Bowery at Bleecker St, tel: 9824052. Nightly. S B, D, F, Q to Broadway/Lafayette St; 6 to Bleecker St. Bus M15, M21, M101, M102. Inexpensive. *The city's best-known rock club. This is where punks and heavy metal fans hang out.*

EAGLE TAVERN 355 W 14th St, between 8th Ave and 9th Ave, tel: 9240275. Opens 0800. Show starts 2030. S A, C, E, L to 14th St/8th Ave. Bus M10, M11, M14. Inexpensive. *Folk venue where you can join in on Mon. Wed. is American folk night, Thu. is for comedy.*

THE RITZ 254 W 54th St, between Broadway and 8th Ave, tel: 5418900. Opens 1900. Shows 2100-0400. S A-D, 1, 9 to 59th St/Columbus Circle. Bus M10, M104. Moderate-Expensive. *The best in rock and R & B, plus unknowns getting their first break.*

SPEAKEASY 107 MacDougal St, tel: 5989670. Nightly. S A-F, S to W 4th St/Washington Sq. Bus M1-M3, M5, M6, M8. Moderate-Expensive. *Folk club with an open stage on Mon. when anyone can perform – the best play again on Tue. Features big stars Wed.-Sat.*

TRAMPS 45 W 21st St, between 5th Ave and 6th Ave, tel: 7277788. Nightly. S N, R to 23rd St. Bus M2, M3, M5-M7. Inexpensive-Moderate. *The best place in New York City to listen to the blues. Rock and pop also get a hearing some nights of the week.*

CENTRAL PARK
CARL SCHURZ PARK
QUEENS
Queensboro Bridge
GREENACRE PARK
PALEY PARK
RIVERSIDE PARK
W 42nd
E 42nd
BRYANT PARK
W 23rd
E 23rd
WASHINGTON SQUARE PARK
Broadway
Fifth Avenue
Park Avenue
MANHATTAN
Roosevelt Island
Hudson River
East River
HOBOKEN
Brooklyn Bridge
WILLIAMSBURG
BATTERY PARK
BROOKLYN
Ellis Island
Liberty Island
PROSPECT PARK

BATTERY PARK Southern tip of Manhattan.
S 1, 9 to Battery Park/South Ferry. Bus M1, M6.
A small park with views of the harbour. See **A-Z**.

BRYANT PARK 42nd St to 6th Ave, behind New York Public Library.
S B, D, F, Q to 42nd St. Bus M5-M7.
A green lung in the centre of Midtown. TKTS booth sells half-price tickets for same-day music and dance performances (see **Theatre**). *See* **A-Z**.

CARL SCHURZ PARK East River, from 84th St to 90th St.
S 4-6 to 86th St. Bus M31, M79, M86.
Watch the ships on the river, sunbathe, play basketball or jog.

CENTRAL PARK From 59th St to 110th St, 5th Ave to Central Park West.
Larger than the principality of Monaco. See **SIGHTSEEING 1**, **WALK 1**, **A-Z**.

GREENACRE PARK 217 E 51st St.
S B, D, F, S to Rockefeller Center. Bus M5-M7.
Pocket handkerchief-sized paved plaza. Calm spot for reading or relaxing.

PALEY PARK E 53rd St, just off 5th Ave.
S E, F to 5th Ave/53rd St. Bus M1-M5.
Tiny 'vest-pocket' park with a waterfall and seats.

PROSPECT PARK Grand Army Plaza, Brooklyn. S D, Q, S to Prospect Park; F to 15th St/Prospect Park; 2, 3 to Grand Army Plaza.
Peace and tranquility of meadows, streams and a lake. Escape the bustle.

RIVERSIDE PARK Hudson River, from 72nd St to 158th St.
S 1, 9 to 110th St, 1, 9 to 116th St. Bus M5.
Manhattan's second-largest park. Take a stroll beside the boat basin.

WASHINGTON SQUARE PARK W 4th St at 5th Ave.
S A-F to W 4th St/Washington Sq. Bus M1-M3, M5, M6, M13, M21.
In the heart of Greenwich Village (see **A-Z**). *See* **A-Z**.

Central Park
Central Park West
Queensboro Br.
West 57th St
East 57th St
QUEENS
Broadway
West 42nd St
East 42nd St
West 34th St
East 34th St
Twelfth Avenue
Eighth Avenue
Fifth Avenue
First Avenue
East River
KHYBER PASS
West 14th St
East 14th St
CUCINA STAGIONALE
SECOND AVENUE DELI
MITALI WEST
TERESA'S
GREAT JONES STREET CAFÉ
East Houston St
TENNESSEE MOUNTAIN
Hudson River
Canal St
TAI HONG LAU
THAILAND
West St
HOBOKEN
Broadway
Brooklyn Br.
BROOKLYN

CUCINA STAGIONALE 275 Bleecker St, between Jones St and Morton St, tel: 9242707. Daily. A-F to W 4th St/Washington Sq. Bus M5, M10. Moderate. *Arrive early or you'll have to queue for the best deal in town on Italian food.*

GREAT JONES STREET CAFÉ 54 Great Jones St, between Broadway and Bowery, tel: 6749304. Daily. B, D, F, 6 to Bleecker St/Lafayette St/Broadway. Bus M1, M3, M5, M6. Moderate. *Popular with young people who patiently wait for delicious Cajun food.*

KHYBER PASS 34 St. Mark's Pl., between 2nd Ave and 3rd Ave, tel: 4730989. Daily. 6 to Astor Pl. Bus M15. Moderate. *Delectable Afghan cuisine, traditional cushions and rugs, great prices.*

MITALI WEST 296 Bleecker St, at corner of 7th Ave and Barrow St, tel: 9891367. Daily. A-F to W 4th St/Washington Sq. Bus M5, M10. Moderate. *Wonderful Indian food, attentive service, and superb value.*

TAI HONG LAU 70 Mott St, between Canal St and Baynard St, tel: 2191431. Daily. J, N, R, 6 to Canal St. Bus M101, M102. Moderate. *Exciting Cantonese dishes served in an elegant setting.*

TENNESSEE MOUNTAIN 143 Spring St, at corner of Wooster St, tel: 4313993. Daily. 6 to Spring St. Bus M1, M6, M8. Moderate. *Authentic 'down-home' barbecues in a charming old clapboard house.*

THAILAND 106 Baynard St at Baxter St below Canal St, tel: 3493132. Daily. J, M, N, R, 6 to Canal St. Bus M101, M102. Moderate. *The best and cheapest Thai food in New York City.*

SECOND AVENUE DELI 156 2nd Ave at 10th St. Daily. 6 to Astor Pl. Bus M15. Inexpensive. *Downtown's favourite Jewish deli.*

TERESA'S 103 1st Ave, between 6th St and 7th St, tel: 2280604. Daily. 6 to Astor Pl. Bus M15. Inexpensive. *Wonderful Polish dishes at exceptional prices.*

Central Park
John's Pizzeria
West Channel
East Channel
Queensboro Bridge
Dawat
West 57th Street
East 57th Street
The Russian Tea Room
Carnegie Deli
Bangkok Cuisine
Peruvian Restaurant
Twelfth Avenue
Tenth Avenue
Eighth Avenue
Fifth Avenue
Third Avenue
First Avenue
Oyster Bar
West 42nd Street
East 42nd Street
Queens Midtown Tunnel
West 34th Street
East 34th Street
Tibetan Kitchen
Hudson River
East River

DAWAT 210 E 58th St, between 2nd Ave and 3rd Ave, tel: 3557555. Daily. N, R, 4-6 to 59th St/Lexington Ave. Bus M101, M102. Expensive. *Good choice of imaginative Indian dishes. Menu devised by Madhur Jaffrey.*

OYSTER BAR Grand Central Station, 42nd St and Vanderbilt Ave, tel: 4906650. 1130-2130 Mon.-Fri. S, 4-7 to Grand Central. Bus M1-M4, M32, M104. Expensive. *Seafood restaurant serving the freshest fish in town. Spectacular setting.*

THE RUSSIAN TEA ROOM 150 W 57th St, near 7th Ave, tel: 2650947. Daily. B, D, E to 7th Ave; N, R to 57th St. Bus M6, M7, M57, M58. Expensive. *Musical celebrities gather under chandeliers to sample caviar and vodka.*

BANGKOK CUISINE 885 8th Ave, between 52nd St and 53rd St, tel: 5816370. Daily. C, E to 50th St/8th Ave; 1, 9 to 50th St/Broadway. Bus M10, M104. Moderate. *One of the best Thai restaurants in the city.*

CARNEGIE DELI 854 7th Ave, between 54th St and 55th St. Daily. B, D, E to 7th Ave; N, R to 57th St. Bus M6, M7. Inexpensive. *An institution. Get to know the real New York in this popular Jewish deli.*

JOHN'S PIZZERIA 408 E 64th St, between 1st Ave and York Ave. Daily. N, R to Lexington Ave; 6 to 68th St/Lexington Ave. Bus M15, M31. Inexpensive. *Delicious thin-crusted pizzas. Dozens of toppings.*

PERUVIAN RESTAURANT 688 10th Ave, at 48th St and 49th St, tel: 5815814. Daily. C, E to 50th St/8th Ave. Bus M11, M27. Inexpensive. *Tasty Peruvian dishes at unbeatable prices.*

TIBETAN KITCHEN 444 3rd Ave, between 30th St and 31st St, tel: 6796286. Closed Sun. 6 to 28th St/Park Ave South. Bus M101, M102. Inexpensive. *Another exotic cuisine in NYC! Well worth trying.*

WEST END GATE
SYLVIA'S RESTAURANT
PATSY'S PIZZA
POPOVER CAFÉ
Central Park
Broadway
Fifth Avenue
Park Avenue
MANHATTAN
ISTANBUL CUISINE
QUEENS
Roosevelt Island
1ST WOK
Queensboro Bridge
Hudson River
J.G. MELON'S
FINE & SCHAPIRO'S
W 42nd
E 42nd
East River
W 23rd
E 23rd
HOBOKEN
Broadway
Brooklyn Bridge
WILLIAMSBURG
BROOKLYN
Ellis Island
Liberty Island

FINE & SCHAPIRO'S 138 W 72nd St, between Broadway and Columbus Ave, tel: 8772874. ■ Daily. S 1-3, 9 to 72nd St/Broadway. Bus M5, M7, M104. ● Moderate. *A classic Jewish restaurant. The best on the West Side.*

ISTANBUL CUISINE 303 E 80th St, between 1st Ave and 2nd Ave, tel: 7446903. ■ Daily. S 6 to 77th St/Lexington Ave. Bus M15. ● Moderate. *Good Turkish cuisine at low prices.*

SYLVIA'S RESTAURANT 328 Lenox Ave, between 126th St and 127th St, tel: 9960660. ■ Daily. S 2, 3 to 125th St/Lenox Ave. Bus M7, M102. Advisable to arrive and depart by taxi. ● Moderate. *A taste of Harlem (see* **A-Z***). Stylish clientele and classic soul food.*

1ST WOK 1374 3rd Ave at 78th St; 1570 3rd Ave, between 88th St and 89th St; 1384 1st Ave at 74th St; 585 2nd Ave at 32nd St. ■ Daily. ● Inexpensive. *Popular branches of a chain of Chinese restaurants serving Szechwan dishes.*

J.G. MELON'S 340 Amsterdam Ave at 76th St; 1291 3rd Ave at 74th St. ■ Daily till late. ● Inexpensive. *Excellent neighbourhood bars serving American-style food.*

PATSY'S PIZZA 2287 1st Ave, between 117th St and 118th St. ■ Daily till late. S 6 to 116th St/Lexington Ave. Bus M101, M102. ● Inexpensive. The *place to go for a pizza if you're in the Harlem (see* **A-Z***) district.*

POPOVER CAFÉ 551 Amsterdam Ave at 87th St. ■ Daily. S 1, 9 to 86th St/Broadway. Bus M7, M11. ● Inexpensive. *Huge American breakfasts and brunches to last you through the day.*

WEST END GATE 2911 Broadway, between 113th St and 114th St. ■ Daily. S 1, 9 to 116th St. Bus M4, M104. ● Inexpensive. *A busy student hang-out with alfresco and bar dining. Straightforward Mexican and Italian food. Jazz most nights.*

Central Park
BLOOMINGDALE'S
ALEXANDER'S
BERGDORF GOODMAN
TIFFANY & CO.
SAKS FIFTH AVENUE
LORD & TAYLOR
MACY'S
BARNEY'S
West 57th Street
East 57th Street
West 42nd Street
East 42nd Street
West 34th Street
East 34th Street
Twelfth Avenue
Tenth Avenue
Eighth Avenue
Fifth Avenue
Third Avenue
First Avenue
Hudson River
East River
West Channel
East Channel
Queensboro Bridge
Queens Midtown Tunnel

Department Stores

See **Opening Times**.

ALEXANDER'S 731 Lexington Ave at E 59th St. S N, R, 4-6 to 59th St/Lexington Ave. Bus M101, M102. *A popular treasure-house full of bargains.*

BARNEY'S 7th Ave and 17th St. S 1, 9 to 18th St/7th Ave. Bus M10. *Ultrasmart men's fashion store in Chelsea. A second store has opened at Madison Ave and 61st St.*

BERGDORF GOODMAN 754 5th Ave, between W 57th St and W 58th St. S N, R to 5th Ave/59th St/60th St; 4-6 to 59th St/Lexington Ave. Bus M1-M5, M32. *Shopping on a grand scale. Carries a large range of fashion collections.*

BLOOMINGDALE'S 1000 3rd Ave at 59th St. S N, R, 4-6 to 59th St/Lexington Ave. Bus M31, M57, M58, M102. *The quintessential New York department store.*

LORD & TAYLOR 424 5th Ave, between 38th St and 39th St. S B, D, F to 42nd St. Bus M1-M5. *Long-established store selling classic American fashions and accessories, household items and antique furniture. Good for browsing.*

MACY'S 151 W 34th St. S B, D, F, N, Q, R, 1-3, 9 to 34th St. Bus M4-M7, M16. *The world's largest department store has absolutely everything for everyone.*

SAKS FIFTH AVENUE 611 5th Ave at 50th St. S B, D, F, Q to Rockefeller Center. Bus M1-M5, M32. *Sophisticated, elegant clothing from top American and European designers.*

TIFFANY & CO. 727 5th Ave at 57th St. S N, R to 5th Ave/59th St/60th St; 4-6 to 59th St/Lexington Ave. Bus M1-M5, M32. *The one and only Tiffany's, selling jewellery, silverware and, surprisingly, some less expensive gift items.*

BILLY MARTIN'S WESTERN WEAR
Central Park West
Central Park
McCREEDY & SCHREIBER
Queensboro Br.
West 57th St
East 57th St
QUEENS
Broadway
GALLERIES LAFAYETTE
West 42nd St
East 42nd St
West 34th St
East 34th St
Twelfth Avenue
Eighth Avenue
Fifth Avenue
First Avenue
East River
BFO
West 14th St
East 14th St
SCREAMING MIMI'S
URBAN OUTFITTERS
CANAL JEAN CO.
East Houston St
FISHKIN
Hudson River
Canal St
West St
HOBOKEN
Broadway
Brooklyn Br.
BROOKLYN

Clothing

See **Opening Times**.

BILLY MARTIN'S WESTERN WEAR 812 Madison Ave at 68th St. S 6 to 68th St/Hunter College/Lexington Ave. Bus M1-M4. *Expensive dude-ranch outfitters. Western clothing for men and women.*

McCREEDY & SCHREIBER 213 E 59th St. S 4-6 to 59th St/ Lexington Ave; N, R to 5th Ave/59th St/60th St. Bus M32, M98, M101, M102. *Every imaginable type of footwear for men, and all at reasonable prices.*

BFO 149 5th Ave at 21st St. S N, R to 23rd St/Broadway. Bus M2, M3, M5. *The best names in menswear at the best prices (more than 50% cheaper than department stores).*

FISHKIN 314 Grand St, near Allan St. S B, D to Grand St. Bus M8, M15. *High-quality clothes (men's and women's) at keen prices.*

URBAN OUTFITTERS 628 Broadway, between Bleecker St and Houston St. S B, D, F to Broadway/Lafayette St; 6 to Bleecker St; N, R to Prince St. Bus M1, M5, M6. *Denim, dungarees, Calvin Klein underwear and affordable mainstream fashion.*

GALERIES LAFAYETTE Trump Tower, 4 E 57th St. S 4-6 to 59th St/Lexington Ave; N, R to 5th Ave/59th St/60th St. Bus M1-M4, M32. *French* haute couture*, tricolors and the Eiffel Tower can all be found in this smart new store for well-heeled women.*

SCREAMING MIMI'S 22 E 4th St and Lafayette St. S 6 to Astor Pl. Bus M1-M3. *For the ostentatious dresser. Clogs, bell-bottoms, handbags and jewellery, all from the '70s.*

CANAL JEAN CO. 504 Broadway, between Spring St and Broome St. S N, R to Prince St. Bus M1, M5, M6. *New and second-hand denim at the lowest prices.*

STAR MAGIC
Central Park West
Central Park
GOTHAM BOOK MART
Queensboro Br.
West 57th St
East 57th St
QUEENS
47TH STREET PHOTO
Broadway
HIRSCH PHOTO
West 42nd St
East 42nd St
West 34th St
East 34th St
Twelfth Avenue
East River
Eighth Avenue
Fifth Avenue
First Avenue
BARNES & NOBLE
West 14th St
East 14th St
STRAND
Hudson River
East Houston St
Canal St
J & R MUSIC WORLD
West St
Broadway
Brooklyn Br.
HOBOKEN
BROOKLYN

Miscellaneous

See **Opening Times**.

BARNES & NOBLE 105 5th Ave at 18th St.
S L, N, R, 4-6 to Union Sq. Bus M2, M3, M5.
The world's largest bookstore. The Sale Annex across the street (at 128 5th Ave) has thousands of discounted books on offer.

47TH STREET PHOTO 67 W 47th St, between 5th Ave and 6th Ave. S B, D, F to Rockefeller Center. Bus M5-M7.
You have to know what you want in this electrical goods store! The staff may be too busy to be of much help, but the prices are good.

GOTHAM BOOK MART 41 W 47th St, between 5th Ave and 6th Ave. S B, D, F to Rockefeller Center. Bus M5-M7.
Crammed full of new and second-hand books, with good film and poetry sections.

HIRSCH PHOTO 699 3rd Ave at 44th St.
S S, 4-7 to Grand Central Station. Bus M101, M102.
Helpful staff and good deals on second-hand cameras.

J & R MUSIC WORLD 23 Park Row, between Ann St and Beekman St. S N, R, 4-6 to Brooklyn Bridge/City Hall. Bus M1, M6, M15, M22, M101.
The latest releases at reasonable prices, though there are few independent labels or imports.

STAR MAGIC 275 Amsterdam Ave at 73rd St.
S 1, 2, 3, 9 to 72nd St/Broadway. Bus M5, M7, M11, M104.
Everything astral and New Age, including telescopes, crystals and hologram jewellery.

STRAND 828 Broadway at 12th St.
S L, N, R, 4-6 to Union Sq./14th St. Bus M6, M7.
The best second-hand bookstore in New York City, with some wonderful bargains.

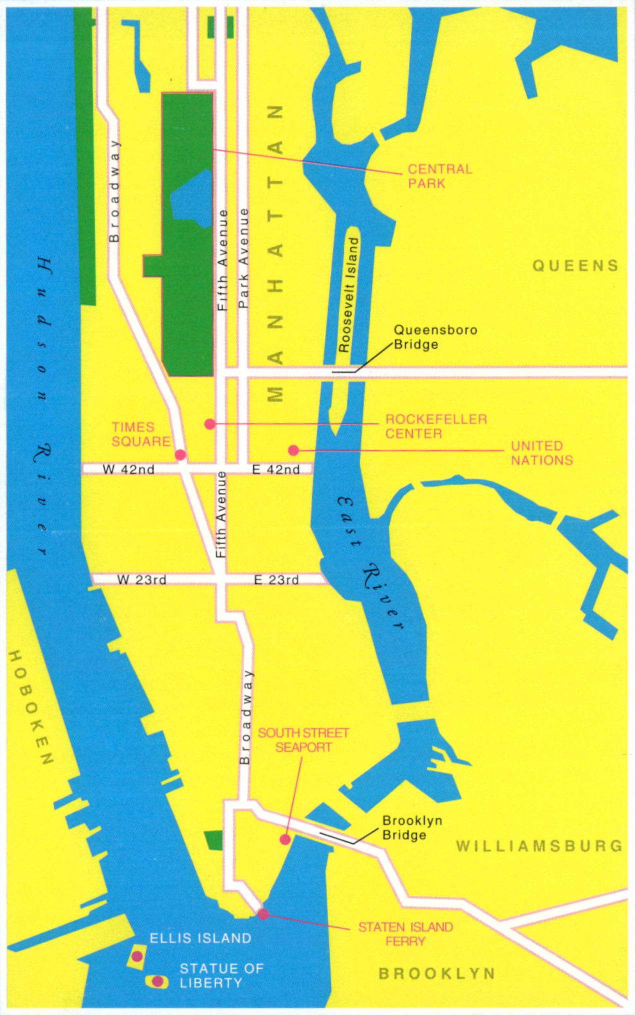
MANHATTAN
CENTRAL PARK
Broadway
Fifth Avenue
Park Avenue
Roosevelt Island
QUEENS
Queensboro Bridge
Hudson River
TIMES SQUARE
ROCKEFELLER CENTER
UNITED NATIONS
W 42nd
E 42nd
East River
W 23rd
E 23rd
HOBOKEN
SOUTH STREET SEAPORT
Brooklyn Bridge
WILLIAMSBURG
STATEN ISLAND FERRY
ELLIS ISLAND
STATUE OF LIBERTY
BROOKLYN

CENTRAL PARK S A, B, C, D, 1, 9 to Columbus Circle; B, N, Q, R to 57th St; N, R to 5th Ave. Bus M1-M4, M30 on 5th Ave; M5-M7 on 59th St; M19, M66, M72, M79, M86, M96 through Central Park. *840 acres of greenery in the middle of Manhattan. See* **PARKS**, **WALK 1**, **A-Z**.

ELLIS ISLAND 0930-1730. S 1, 9 to South Ferry. Bus M1, M6. Circle Line Ferry every 30 min (0930-1500) from Battery Park. Museum Free. Ferry (joint ticket for Statue of Liberty – see below) Moderate. *Former immigration centre and gateway to America for the 12 million 'huddled masses yearning to breathe free'. See* **A-Z**.

ROCKEFELLER CENTER 48th St to 52nd St, 5th Ave to 7th Ave. S B, D, F to Rockefeller Center. Bus M1-M7. *A prestigious 22 acre complex featuring 19 Art Deco buildings. See* **A-Z**.

SOUTH STREET SEAPORT South St. S J, M, Z, 2, 3, 4, 5, to Fulton St; A, C to Broadway/Nassau. *The 19thC port district now has bars, shops and restaurants. See* **A-Z**.

STATEN ISLAND FERRY South Ferry. S 1, 9 to South Ferry. Bus M1, M6. 50c return (avoid at rush hours). *Views of Manhattan, the Statue of Liberty and Ellis Island. See* **Staten Island**.

STATUE OF LIBERTY 0930-1730. S 1, 9 to South Ferry. Bus M1, M6. Circle Line Ferry every 30 min (0930-1500) from Battery Park. Statue Free. Ferry (joint ticket for Ellis Island – see above) Moderate. *Symbol of American freedom and the American Dream. See* **A-Z**.

TIMES SQUARE 42nd St to 47th St, Broadway to 7th Ave. S N, R, S, 1-3, 7, 9, to Times Sq., A-F to 42nd St. Bus M6, M7. *The former home of* The New York Times *(see* **Newspapers***). See* **A-Z**.

UNITED NATIONS 1st Ave, between 42nd St and 48th St. 0915-1645. S S, 4-7 to 42nd St/Grand Central Station. Bus M15, M27, M42, M50, M104. Moderate. No preschool-age children allowed. *Famous complex where global issues are discussed. See* **A-Z**.

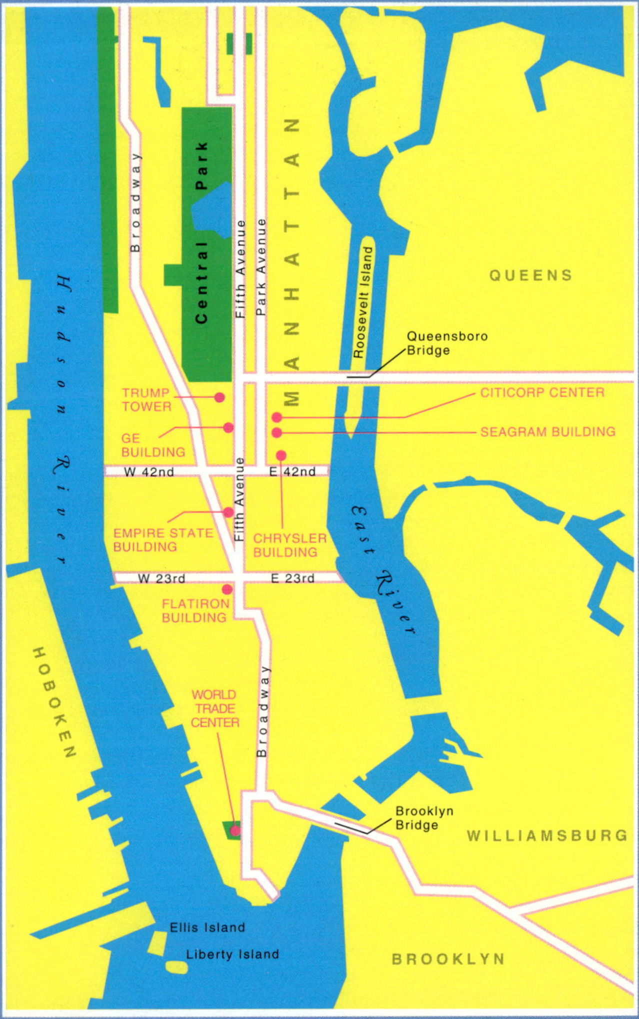

Broadway
Central Park
Fifth Avenue
Park Avenue
MANHATTAN
Roosevelt Island
QUEENS
Queensboro Bridge
Hudson River
TRUMP TOWER
GE BUILDING
CITICORP CENTER
SEAGRAM BUILDING
W 42nd
E 42nd
EMPIRE STATE BUILDING
CHRYSLER BUILDING
East River
W 23rd
E 23rd
FLATIRON BUILDING
HOBOKEN
WORLD TRADE CENTER
Broadway
Brooklyn Bridge
WILLIAMSBURG
Ellis Island
Liberty Island
BROOKLYN

CHRYSLER BUILDING Lexington Ave at 42nd St.
S 4-7 to Grand Central Station. Bus M1-M4.
Spectacular Art Deco skyscraper. See **A-Z**.

CITICORP CENTER Lexington Ave at 53rd St.
S E, F to 53rd St/Lexington Ave; 6 to 51st St. Bus M101, M102.
New York City's fifth-tallest building, with a distinctive slanted roof and an atrium. See **A-Z**.

EMPIRE STATE BUILDING 5th Ave at 34th St. S B, D, F, N, R to 34th St/Herald Sq.; 6 to 33rd St/Park Ave South. Bus M1-M5. *An Art Deco masterpiece with observation areas on floors 86 and 102. See* **A-Z**.

FLATIRON BUILDING 5th Ave and Broadway. S F, N, R to 23rd St. Bus M2, M3, M5-M7. *Built in 1902, this wedge-shaped landmark was one of the earliest buildings to be constructed with a steel frame. See* **Madison Square**.

GE BUILDING 30 Rockefeller Plaza, between 49th St and 50th St. S B, D, F to Rockefeller Center. Bus M5-M7. *The home of NBC Studios and Radio City Music Hall (see* MUSIC VENUES*). See* **Rockefeller Center**.

SEAGRAM BUILDING 375 Park Ave, between 52nd St and 53rd St. S E, F to 53rd St/Lexington Ave. Bus M1-M4, M32, M101, M102. *A bronze and glass building by Philip Johnson and Mies Van der Rohe. See* **A-Z**.

TRUMP TOWER 725 5th Ave at 57th St. S 4-6 to 59th St/Lexington Ave, N, R to 5th Ave/59th St/60th St. Bus M1-M4. *A spectacular building. The extravagant atrium houses exclusive shops. See* **A-Z**.

WORLD TRADE CENTER World Trade Center Plaza, Church St. S A, C, E to Chambers St/World Trade Center; 2, 3 to Park Pl. Bus M1, M6, M10, M22. *The twin towers dominate the city. No. 2 boasts the highest open-air observation deck in the world (closed in bad weather). See* **A-Z**.

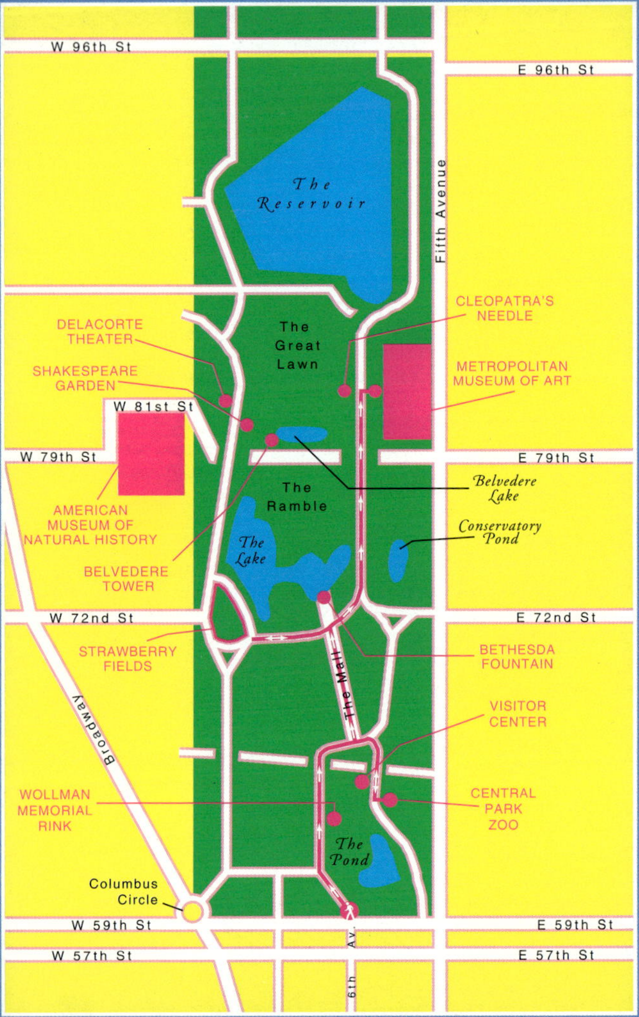

W 96th St
E 96th St
The Reservoir
Fifth Avenue
CLEOPATRA'S NEEDLE
DELACORTE THEATER
The Great Lawn
SHAKESPEARE GARDEN
METROPOLITAN MUSEUM OF ART
W 81st St
W 79th St
E 79th St
Belvedere Lake
The Ramble
AMERICAN MUSEUM OF NATURAL HISTORY
Conservatory Pond
The Lake
BELVEDERE TOWER
W 72nd St
E 72nd St
STRAWBERRY FIELDS
BETHESDA FOUNTAIN
The Mall
Broadway
VISITOR CENTER
CENTRAL PARK ZOO
WOLLMAN MEMORIAL RINK
The Pond
Columbus Circle
W 59th St
E 59th St
W 57th St
E 57th St
6th Av.

WALK 1

Duration: 1 hr 30 min, excluding boat trips, gallery visits, etc. While the park is generally safe during daylight hours, you should avoid straying from the main thoroughfares. See **PARKS, SIGHTSEEING 1**, **A-Z**.

Begin at the entrance to the park on 59th St and 6th Ave. Follow the avenue into the park where it veers to the left, passing The Pond, on your right, and continuing past the Wollman Memorial Rink. Turn right towards East Drive and call in at The Dairy, now a visitor centre, where you can obtain maps and information. Once on East Drive, turn left to reach Central Park Zoo (see **A-Z**); the Children's Zoo is just north of the main zoo. Turn right up East Drive to The Mall, a long, tree-lined path leading to the beautiful Bethesda Fountain, and, just beyond that, The Lake. Turn left before the fountain and walk towards the Dakota Building (see **A-Z**) on 72nd St, across from which is Strawberry Fields, the 2.5 acre memorial to John Lennon, planted with many trees, shrubs and flowers sent as gifts of peace from other countries. Return to the fountain and take a left turn to the Loeb Boathouse, where there are rowing boats and bicycles for hire (see **Bicycle Hire**). East of The Lake and boathouse is the Conservatory Pond, with statues of Alice in Wonderland and Hans Christian Andersen, where the young, and young at heart, sail model yachts. Children's storytelling sessions are held here during summer (1100 Wed. & Sat.), and you can hire rowing boats. Walking northwards on East Drive you will see The Ramble to the left just beyond The Lake, a wooded hill much favoured by bird-watchers and muggers. Avoid going in! Carry on along the same route past Belvedere Lake. The 'medieval' Belvedere Tower stands to the southwest of the lake across from The Ramble and overlooks the north part of the park. (The Shakespeare Garden is just to the west of it, and the Delacorte Theater – see **Theatre** – is to the north.) Continuing in the same direction, you soon come to Cleopatra's Needle, the twin of that in London, donated by the Khedive of Egypt in 1881. The Great Lawn beyond is much used for games. The Metropolitan Museum of Art (see **A-Z**) stands on the right. There is little of interest beyond here other than The Reservoir, beloved of joggers, and the Conservatory Garden. Relax in the Met's café, on the south side of the building, before leaving the park by the 72nd St exit.

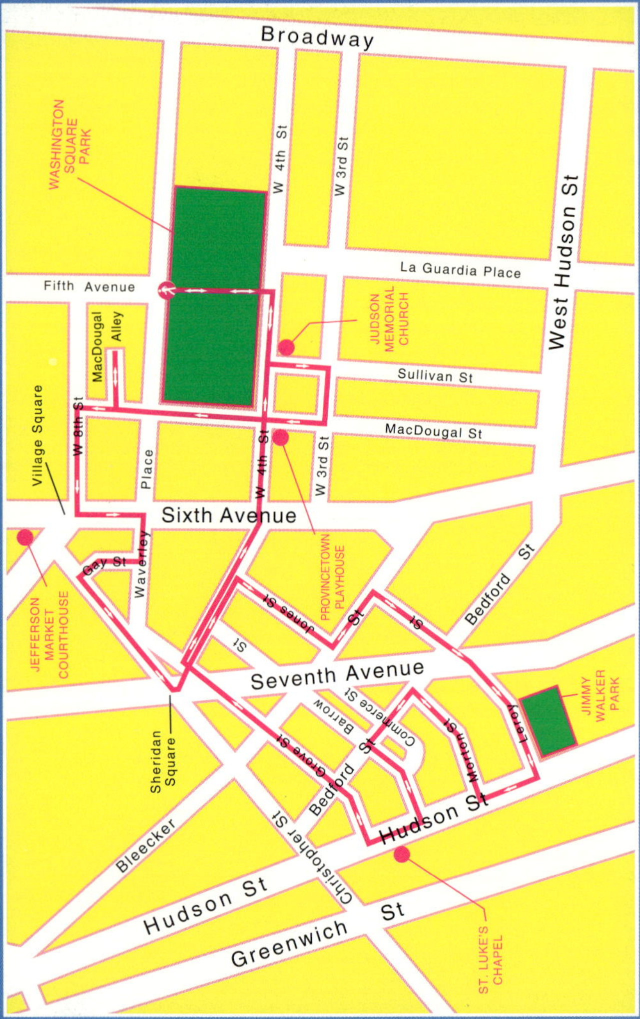
Broadway
W 4th St
W 3rd St
West Hudson St
WASHINGTON SQUARE PARK
La Guardia Place
Fifth Avenue
JUDSON MEMORIAL CHURCH
MacDougal Alley
Sullivan St
Village Square
W 8th St
MacDougal St
Place
W 4th St
W 3rd St
Sixth Avenue
PROVINCETOWN PLAYHOUSE
Gay St
Waverley
JEFFERSON MARKET COURTHOUSE
Jones St
St
Bedford St
St
Seventh Avenue
JIMMY WALKER PARK
Commerce St
Barrow
Morton St
Leroy
Sheridan Square
Grove St
Bedford
St
Hudson St
Bleecker
Christopher St
Hudson St
Greenwich St
ST. LUKE'S CHAPEL

Greenwich Village

Duration: 1 hr-1hr 30 min. See CITY DISTRICTS, **A-Z**.

Start at Washington Square Arch (see PARKS, **A-Z**) at the beginning of 5th Ave. The square is the spiritual epicentre of the Village, always alive with every kind of activity imaginable, from a classical concert to kids dousing themselves in the fountain. Cross to the south side of the park. Turn right as you leave and you will see the Judson Memorial Church on your left. Turn left into Sullivan St, then right into W 3rd St, and then right again into MacDougal St, passing the Provincetown Playhouse on your left. Continue along MacDougal St as it becomes Washington Sq. West (see the chess players in the southwest corner of the park) and then MacDougal St again. Look down MacDougal Alley to see the little mews belonging to the houses on the square, which were formerly stables. Return to MacDougal St and turn left onto W 8th St (lined with shoe shops), heading towards 6th Ave, until you arrive at the Village Square dominated by the Jefferson Market Courthouse (now a library). Turn left onto 6th Ave, lined with shops selling incense and second-hand books, right into Waverley Pl. and then right again into Gay St. Turn left onto Christopher St, the heart of the Village's gay community, and walk past Waverley Pl. to Sheridan Sq. at 7th Ave. Turn left into W 4th St and stroll past the shops and cafés to Jones St. Follow Jones St, turn left onto Bleecker St, an Italian district known for its *trattorie* and pastry shops, then right onto Leroy St. West of Bleecker St are some of the loveliest leafy residential streets in NYC. Continue along Leroy St across 7th Ave to St. Luke's Pl. and the Jimmy Walker Park, which commemorates a flamboyant Jazz Age mayor of New York who lived at No. 6 St. Luke's Pl. (Theodore Dreiser wrote *An American Tragedy* at No. 16.) Turn right into Hudson St and right again into Morton St, which brings you to Bedford St. Both Edna St. Vincent Millay, the feminist poet, and John Barrymore, the '20s matinée idol, are thought to have lived at No. 75 1/2, reputedly the narrowest house in New York City. A left turn onto Barrow St and then a right on Hudson St brings you to St. Luke's Chapel. Turn right from here into Grove St, a peaceful area contrasting sharply with the bustle of Bleecker St, and continue along it to W 4th St, past 19thC Federal-style Grove Court. Follow W 4th St across 6th Ave back to Washington Sq.

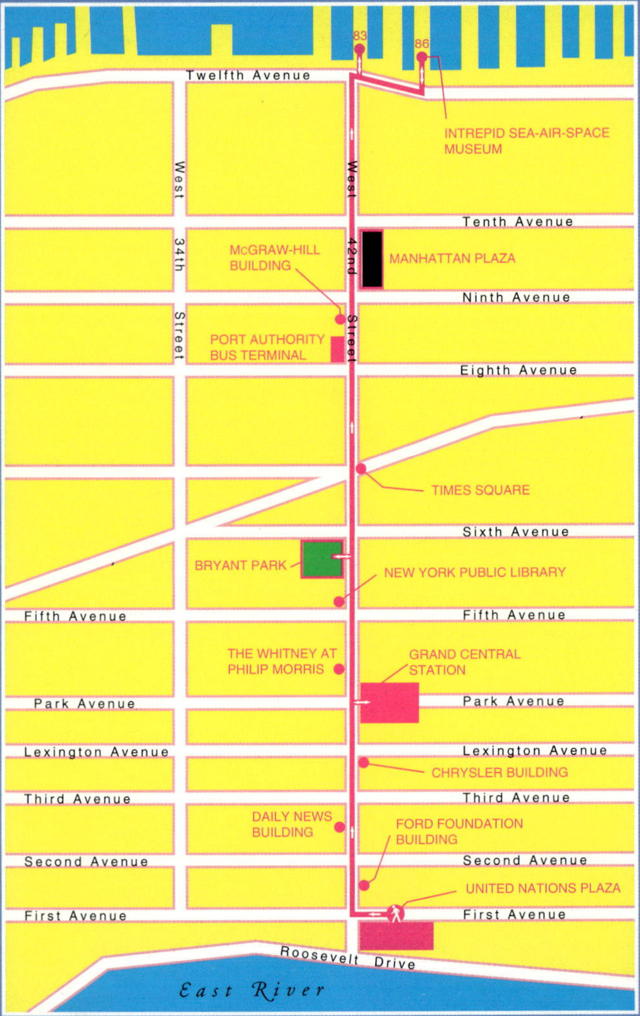
83
86
Twelfth Avenue
INTREPID SEA-AIR-SPACE MUSEUM
West 34th Street
West 42nd Street
Tenth Avenue
McGRAW-HILL BUILDING
MANHATTAN PLAZA
Ninth Avenue
PORT AUTHORITY BUS TERMINAL
Eighth Avenue
TIMES SQUARE
Sixth Avenue
BRYANT PARK
NEW YORK PUBLIC LIBRARY
Fifth Avenue
Fifth Avenue
THE WHITNEY AT PHILIP MORRIS
GRAND CENTRAL STATION
Park Avenue
Park Avenue
Lexington Avenue
Lexington Avenue
CHRYSLER BUILDING
Third Avenue
Third Avenue
DAILY NEWS BUILDING
FORD FOUNDATION BUILDING
Second Avenue
Second Avenue
UNITED NATIONS PLAZA
First Avenue
First Avenue
Roosevelt Drive
East River

42nd Street

Duration: 1 hr 30 min. Take Bus M42, which runs the length of 42nd St, to the United Nations headquarters.

Start at UN Plaza outside the United Nations headquarters (see **A-Z**) on 1st Ave and turn onto 42nd St. Head due west until you reach the Ford Foundation Building (see **A-Z**), on the right, which has a fine, leafy atrium. Continuing in the same direction, you come to the Daily News Building (see **A-Z**), on the left-hand side, where *Superman* was filmed. Your next stop should be at the junction with Lexington Ave, where you can admire the splendid Art Deco Chrysler Building (see **A-Z**). Look up to see the steel gargoyles protruding from the tapering edifice. The Grand Hyatt Hotel, with its restaurant leaning out over the street, and then Grand Central Station (see **A-Z**) are just a little further on. This part of 42nd St has many fine Beaux Arts buildings, such as the Bowery Savings Bank across from the station, which have elaborately decorated lobbies you can visit. The Whitney at Philip Morris is a branch of the Whitney Museum of American Art (see **A-Z**). It has a small picture gallery and sculpture court, as well as an espresso bar which is a good place for a breather. Further along, at the corner of 5th Ave, is the New York Public Library (see **A-Z**). The green sward of Bryant Park (see **A-Z**), with a TKTS booth for music and dance events (see **Theatre**), is just past the library on the same side of the street. At the northwest corner of the park a digital display informs Americans of their country's national debt. Continue west to Times Square (see **A-Z**) and enjoy the sight of one of the busiest and most famous crossroads in the world. A nonstop diet of electronic news pumps around the central building, which also displays a gigantic CNN news screen. Increased police presence makes the area feel less threatening than it did a few years ago. On the north side of the square is a TKTS booth selling discounted theatre tickets. Continue past the pornography cinemas between 7th Ave and 8th Ave, and the Port Authority Bus Terminal. Note the old McGraw-Hill Building on the left, a bit further on, which has been designated a city landmark. The Holy Cross Church (see **Duffy Square**) opposite is the oldest building on 42nd St (there is a statue at the north side of Times Square of its former pastor, Father Duffy). If you have time, take a detour along 9th Ave into the area of Paddy's Market (between 38th St

Chrysler Building

and 44th St), which is no longer a true market, but contains a wealth of different food shops. This is the site of the Ninth Avenue International Festival (see **Events**). Returning to the stretch of 42nd St between 9th Ave and 10th Ave, you come to Theater Row, housing many off-Broadway theatres, and Manhattan Plaza, the residence of artists and actors. Continue to the end of 42nd St and turn up 12th Ave to the end of 43rd St, where you'll find Pier 83, the departure point for a Circle Line cruise round the island of Manhattan (see **Ferries**). Turn northwards up 12th Ave to Pier 86, site of the *Intrepid* Sea-Air-Space Museum, an aircraft carrier displaying fighter planes, prototype models and other paraphernalia of war (1000-1700 Wed.-Sun., daily in summer; Expensive).

Fifth Avenue

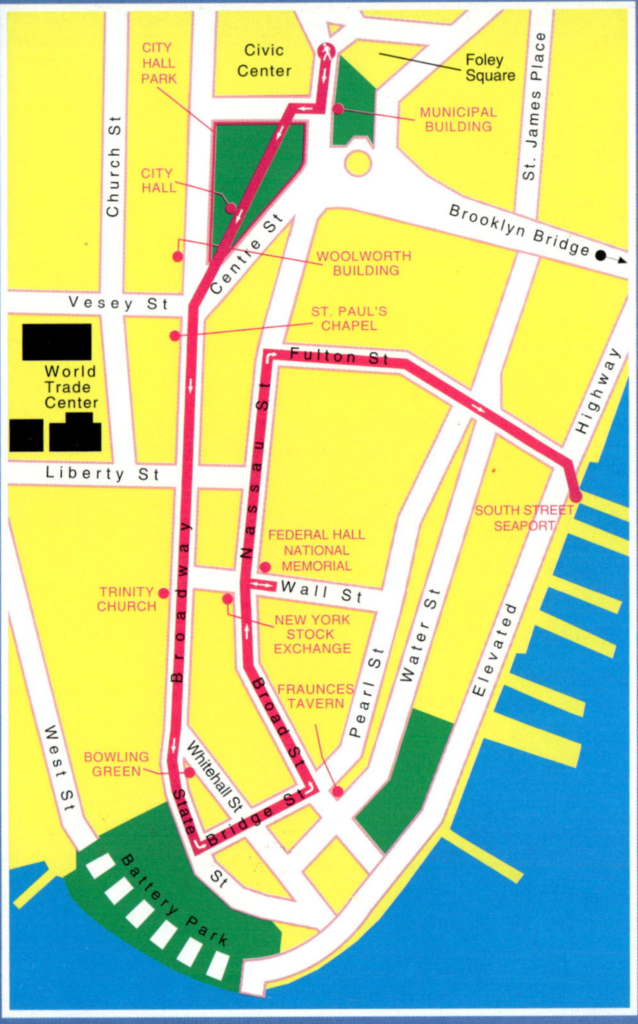
CITY HALL PARK
Civic Center
Foley Square
MUNICIPAL BUILDING
St. James Place
Church St
CITY HALL
Brooklyn Bridge
Centre St
WOOLWORTH BUILDING
Vesey St
ST. PAUL'S CHAPEL
World Trade Center
Fulton St
Highway
Liberty St
Nassau St
SOUTH STREET SEAPORT
FEDERAL HALL NATIONAL MEMORIAL
Wall St
TRINITY CHURCH
NEW YORK STOCK EXCHANGE
Broadway
Water St
Elevated
Pearl St
FRAUNCES TAVERN
Broad St
West St
BOWLING GREEN
Whitehall St
State St
Bridge St
Battery Park

Heritage Trail

Duration: 1 hr. A 3 mile walk along the Heritage Trail. The best time to do it is during the day on a weekday when you can experience the pace of Downtown city life. Take Train 6 to Brooklyn Bridge station.

Start at Foley Sq. in the Civic Center (see **A-Z**) and walk south to the Municipal Building (crowned by the statue of Civic Fame) at No. 1 Centre St. Walk past City Hall through City Hall Park to Broadway (see **A-Z**). Continue down Broadway to the Woolworth Building (see **A-Z**) and admire the humorous caricatures of the owner, architect and builder in the lobby. Continue south along Broadway past St. Paul's Chapel (see **A-Z**) and Trinity Church (see **A-Z**) until you reach the Bowling Green (see **A-Z**), at the northern end of which stands the aggressive bronze bull sculpture by Arturo DiModica, created in response to the stockmarket crash of 1987 and illustrating the vitality of the American people in adverse times. Battery Park (see **A-Z**) across the road contains Castle Clinton (see **A-Z**) which looks out towards the harbour. Keep going along the adjoining State St and then turn left along Bridge St to the Fraunces Tavern (see **A-Z**) at the corner of Pearl St and Broad St. It contains a museum on the War of American Independence, as well as a restaurant which serves excellent breakfasts. Turn onto Broad St, going in a northerly direction, and follow it to Wall St, where you can visit the New York Stock Exchange (see **A-Z**). Continue north past the Federal Hall National Memorial (see **A-Z**) and along Nassau St to the Federal Reserve Bank at Liberty St. The bank was built in Renaissance style in 1924 and is where the world's nations store and exchange gold in order to maintain a balance of trade. The gold is kept in five underground floors. Continue until you reach Fulton St, then turn right into it and head for the East River (see **A-Z**). You are now in the heart of the South Street Seaport (see **A-Z**).

World Trade Center & Chinatown

American Museum of Natural History: Unfortunately the dinosaur section, with its famous dinosaur fossils, is presently undergoing restoration (1993), though massive re-created monsters fill the main hall. However, there are many other attractions, including the Hall of Meteorites, which houses the Star of India, the largest blue sapphire in the world (563 carats), and the Hall of Ocean Life, containing a 94 ft-long suspended replica of a blue whale. The Hall of African Mammals on the second floor is home to dioramas of elephants, lions, zebras and giraffes, while the third floor has the Naturemax Theater, with the largest indoor screen in New York (it's four storeys high), which shows documentaries. The Hayden Planetarium (see **A-Z**) is adjacent to the museum. See CHILDREN.

Astors: Along with the Rockefellers (see **A-Z**) and the Vanderbilts (see **A-Z**), the Astors are famous as one of the richest and most powerful families in New York. The founding member was John Jacob Astor (1886-1971), a German immigrant who made his fortune in the fur trade.

Audubon Terrace: W 155th St and Broadway. This fine terrace designed by Charles Pratt Huntington and built in 1908 is home to several museums, including the Museum of the American Indian (see MUSEUMS 2) and the Hispanic Society of America (see MUSEUMS 3).

Avenue of the Americas: The official name for 6th Ave. Most New Yorkers refer to it as 6th Ave, and this guidebook follows their example.

Battery Park: The park lies at the tip of Manhattan and offers good views of the harbour. The ferry terminals (see **Ferries**) for all the islands are situated here, including the Staten Island ferry (see SIGHTSEEING 1). The battery was used to defend the island of Manhattan against the British. See PARKS, WALK 4.

Big Apple, The: Jazz musicians in the '20s and '30s coined New York's nickname: when you played in New York City you'd hit the big

time and reached the shiniest apple 'at the top of the success tree'. The name went out of fashion until the '70s, when it was reintroduced by the New York Convention and Visitors Bureau (see **Tourist Information**), in what it claims as 'the world's most famous and effective city tourist promotion'.

Bowery: This street, named after *bouwerie* (Dutch for 'farm'), stretches from Canal St, just above Chinatown (see **A-Z**), east of Little Italy (see **A-Z**) and Greenwich Village (see **A-Z**) to Cooper Sq. Its notoriety goes back to its vaudeville days, when the 'Bowery Boys' robbed the patrons of dance hall and bars. The area now has a large vagrant population. Look out for the Savings Bank at No. 130 which makes a definite architectural statement about the nature of financial security, it being in the form of a Roman basilica with a 160 ft-long banking hall and marble mosaic floors.

Bowling Green: Broadway at Battery Pl. This area has been a bowling green, a cattle market and a parade ground in its time. It is also the legendary spot where Peter Minuit traded $24 worth of trinkets to the Indians for the rights to Manhattan. The building behind the green is the old Customs House which is decorated with sculptures of the continents of Europe, Africa, Asia and America. See **WALK 4**.

Broadway: The USA's longest street, stretching 146 miles to Albany. Within New York City, Broadway is the home of the Theater District (see **CITY DISTRICTS**), at the heart of which lies Times Square (see **A-Z**). See **WALK 4**.

Bronx, The: The borough to the north of Manhattan across the Harlem River is the home of the Bronx Zoo (see **A-Z**), Edgar Allan Poe Cottage (where the novelist lived from 1846 to 1848), New York Botanical Garden (see **A-Z**), City Island (which looks like a coastal fishing village) and Belmont. There is also a lively Italian market on Arthur Ave.

Bronx Zoo: The world's largest zoo, with almost 4000 animals inhabiting 265 acres. Jungle World is the naturalistic habitat for Asian wildlife which can be visited by monorail on the Bengali Express. Don't miss the feeding times for the pelicans, crocodiles, sea lions, penguins and big cats. Try to visit the zoo in spring or summer when it is at its best. The easiest way to the zoo is by subway. See **CHILDREN**.

Brooklyn: Although in the process of becoming 'yuppified', this borough has a lot to offer visitors. There is the Brooklyn Academy of Music (see **A-Z**), the Brooklyn Children's Museum (see **CHILDREN**), the Brooklyn Museum (see **A-Z**) in Prospect Park (see **PARKS**), and Coney Island (see **A-Z**). A walk across the magnificent Brooklyn Bridge (see **A-Z**) brings you to the fashionable district of Brooklyn Heights, full of old American houses. From here the subway will take you to other parts such as Carroll Gardens, Cobble Hill and Prospect Park (avoid Bedford-Stuyvesant, a notorious ghetto). Brooklyn has a population of 2.25 million, the largest of New York's five boroughs.

Brooklyn Botanic Garden

Brooklyn Academy of Music (BAM): The world-famous academy stages a Next Wave Festival of avant-garde performances in dance and music every autumn. In the spring there is a Black Dance Festival featuring diverse forms of music and movement. See **MUSIC VENUES**.

Brooklyn Botanic Garden: 1000 Washington Ave. These attractive gardens adjoining the Brooklyn Museum (see **A-Z**) include a Japanese Hill, a Pond Garden, a Shakespeare Garden and a Fragrance Garden for the blind. 0800-1800 Tue.-Fri., 1000-1800 Sat. & Sun.; Free.

Brooklyn Bridge: This was New York City's first suspension bridge, designed by John A. Roebling and completed in 1883. The central span is 1595 ft long and the two Gothic-style towers 277 ft high. The best way to see the bridge is to take subways A or C to High St/Brooklyn Bridge and to walk back across it along the pedestrian deck above the road to Manhattan.

Brooklyn Museum: In almost any other city in the world the Brooklyn Museum would rate as a top attraction. But in New York there's too much competition, not least from the unequalled

Metropolitan Museum of Art (see **A-Z**). The reason why a museum of such size and breadth should exist so far from the city centre is explained by the fact that the borough of Brooklyn was a separate city until 1898. Of the five floors of art, the Egyptian Collection and reconstructed period rooms from around the world are the outstanding highlights. Italian Renaissance painters, Americans and French Impressionists are best represented in the picture galleries. Major refurbishment may be under way. Due to funding cuts, some galleries may be closed. Tel: 718-6385000 in advance if you want to see something specific. See **MUSEUMS 1**.

Bryant Park: This park behind the New York Public Library (see **A-Z**) is named after William Cullen Bryant, the editor of the *New York Post* who campaigned for the establishment of Central Park (see **A-Z**) when the site it now occupies was a swamp. See **PARKS**, **WALK 3**.

Carnegie Hall: This grand concert hall, seating 2800 people, was built in 1883 with help from the famous Scottish-American industrialist Andrew Carnegie. The hall came close to being demolished after the Lincoln Center (see **A-Z**) opened but its acoustics have been improved and the hall is now a preserved building. See **MUSIC VENUES**.

Cast-iron Buildings: These were built in the period from the 1850s to the 1890s, when it was discovered that it was easier to construct buildings of cast iron, thin iron columns being capable of bearing as much weight as thick stone walls. Elaborate decoration was already a feature of stonework and again it was found to be easier and cheaper to employ it in the moulding of cast iron. The best of the cast-iron buildings are situated on Greene St in SoHo (see **A-Z**).

Castle Clinton: This fort was originally sited out in the harbour in order to provide crossfire for the battery which gave Battery Park (see **A-Z**) its name. The stretch of water between them was filled in and now the castle is in Battery Park itself. Prior to its restoration as a fort, and its designation as a national monument, it served as a concert venue, an immigration centre and an aquarium. See **WALK 4**.

Central Park

Central Park: New Yorkers owe the existence of Central Park to the campaigning William Cullen Bryant (see **Bryant Park**), and the architectural genius of Frederick Law Olmstead (see **A-Z**) and Calvert Vaux. Nearly 20% of the park's area consists of water and you can visit a model-boat pond, or go out on The Lake in a rowing boat or even a Venetian gondola. For theatre buffs there is the Delacorte Theater which hosts the free Shakespeare in the Park Festival during the summer (see **Events**, **Theatre**). Other attractions include Central Park Zoo (see **A-Z**), ice-skating rinks, horse-riding trails, jogging routes, hansom cab rides, trolley rides (see **Tours**), pedal carriages and Urban Park Ranger walks. The park is at its heady and invigorating best on a summer weekend, when it's easy to spend a whole day soaking up the atmosphere of what seems like half the city at play. Salsa rhythms may be drifting over from a Summerstage concert as an eclectic collection of cyclists, joggers and roller-bladers fill the thoroughfares on their park circuits. See **PARKS**, **SIGHTSEEING 1**, **WALK 1**.

Central Park Zoo: Reopened in 1988 after a $35 million renovation, the zoo now boasts three ecological areas – the Tropics Zone, the Temperate Territory and the Polar Circle – all set round a central formal garden. Walkways connect the indoor and outdoor habitats with the Sea Lion Pool in the middle. The zoo is often crowded. See **WALK 1**.

Chelsea: This area, stretching from 14th St to 34th St and from 6th Ave to the Hudson River (see **A-Z**), has little of interest for the visitor apart from the Chelsea Hotel (see **A-Z**). It is mostly a residential district but has an array of bars and restaurants along 8th Ave. It can be reached on Buses M5-M7, M10 and M11, and subways A-C, E and F to 23rd St.

Chelsea Hotel: 222 W 23rd St. The hotel's literary associations began when Chelsea (see **A-Z**) was New York's theatre district. Some famous writers and artists, such as Mark Twain, Tennessee Williams, Brendan Behan, Bob Dylan and Andy Warhol, have lived and worked in this Gothic-style pile built in 1884, with its wrought-iron balconies and elaborate staircase.

Chinatown: A small but ever-growing area, of which Mott St is the main thoroughfare. Hard up against Bowery (see **A-Z**) and the Civic Center (see **A-Z**), Chinatown epitomizes the distinct ethnic community divisions of Manhattan; dustbin vans have 'Chinatown' written on them in Chinese script, and pagodas sit on top of phone kiosks. Most people visit the area in search of cheap food as there are well over 100 restaurants to choose from, and as many food shops. See **CITY DISTRICTS**.

Chrysler Building: Completed in 1930, for a short time before the Empire State Building (see **A-Z**) was finished, this was New York's tallest building (77 storeys), and many feel that, with its Art Deco crown, it is still the city's finest. The architecture is based on car designs from the 1920s. The opulent lobby is the only part of the building open to the public. See **SIGHTSEEING 2, WALK 3**.

Citicorp Center: The center's steeply-angled roof was intended to provide solar power for the building but unfortunately it doesn't work. The three-storey atrium, decorated with tumbling greenery, houses an

excellent shopping area with restaurants. The little Lutheran Church of St. Peter (see **CHURCHES**) has a chapel with jazz vespers at 1700 on Sun, followed by concerts at 1900. See **SIGHTSEEING 2**.

Civic Center: Situated in City Hall Park, the Civic Center comprises the Georgian-style City Hall, a beautiful New York City landmark dating from 1812 and housing the mayor's office and historic exhibits, the Woolworth Building (see **A-Z**), facing City Hall, and the Tweed Courthouse behind it, which is named after the notorious NYC boss who ran the city for his own gain in the 1860s and '70s. See **WALK 4**.

Cloisters: This is the medieval collection of the Metropolitan Museum of Art (see **A-Z**). Exhibited in a dramatic setting high above the Hudson River (see **A-Z**) at the northern tip of Manhattan, it consists of parts of five medieval monasteries transported brick by brick from Europe and reconstructed here as examples of 12th-15thC Gothic architecture. Highlights include a Romanesque chapel, the Unicorn tapestries, stained-glass windows, and peaceful gardens with vistas over the Hudson River. See **MUSEUMS 1**.

Cloisters

Coney Island: Off South Brooklyn, this is not as popular as it once was, but it still has Nathan's, where the hot dog originated, and the Astroland Amusement Park. Other attractions include the recently-expanded New York Aquarium, which has beluga whales, sea lions, seals, penguins, dolphin shows and a touch-it tank (1000-1700; Moderate), Brighton and Manhattan beaches, and the boardwalk. Fun and crowded on a hot summer weekend, Coney Island can be deserted on a cloudy weekday. Take subways B, D, F and N to Coney Island.

Cooper-Hewitt Museum: The museum is in the former mansion of the Scottish-American industrialist Andrew Carnegie, which provides an ideal setting for the national design collection of textiles (some up to 3000 years old), jewellery, furniture, and architectural designs and drawings. Lectures, classes, concerts and exhibitions are held here. See MUSEUMS 2.

Daily News Building: 220 E 42nd St, between 2nd Ave and 3rd Ave. Designed in 1930 by Raymond Hood and the home of *The Daily News*, this building is probably better known as the offices of *The Daily Planet*, the newspaper which employed Clark Kent and Lois Lane in *Superman*. A globe does actually exist; it is in the lobby along with clocks displaying the time around the world. See WALK 3.

Dakota Building: 1 W 72nd St. The name of this building derives from a joke it prompted in 1884 when it was built – that it lay so far north it was actually in Dakota territory. The joke resulted in the building's owner, Edward Clark, having Wild West emblems added to the façades. It was the setting for the film *Rosemary's Baby* and the scene of John Lennon's assassination in 1980. See WALK 1.

Downtown: Anything south of 14th St, the oldest part of Manhattan, constitutes Downtown. However, in directions, it can also refer to anywhere south of where you are at present. See **Orientation**.

Duffy Square: This square, situated in the north part of Times Square (see **A-Z**) between 46th St and 47th St, is named after Father

Francis P. Duffy, the pastor of Holy Cross Church in 42nd St (see **WALK 3**). It contains his statue as well as that of George M. Cohan, the song and dance man, who wrote *Yankee Doodle Dandy* and *Give My Regards to Broadway*. The TKTS ticket booth is also situated here (see **Theatre**).

East River: Flowing down from Long Island Sound, the river divides the borough of Queens (see **A-Z**), on Long Island, from the Bronx (see **A-Z**) on the mainland. Further south, it divides Manhattan from Brooklyn (see **A-Z**) and Queens (see **A-Z**).

East Village: This district has seen many changes since it was Peter Stuyvesant's estate. Astors (see **A-Z**) and Vanderbilts (see **A-Z**) lived here in the 19thC before the rising population of Eastern European immigrants transformed it into 'Little Ukraine'. In the 1950s the Beat poets formed an artists' colony here. It is now perhaps New York's liveliest, most avant-garde district. Its more respectable side stretches between Ave A and 3rd Ave, particularly around St. Mark's Pl. East of Ave A lies Alphabet City, whose backstreets are fascinating but poverty-ridden. Tompkins Sq. has recently been made more salubrious by the eviction of its homeless community. See **CITY DISTRICTS**.

Ellis Island: The significance of Ellis Island in US history cannot be overstated. From 1892 to 1954 12 million immigrants landed here. Their descendants have been calculated to make up 40% of the US population. At vast expense, the main building has been restored and converted into a fine museum. There are numerous displays humanizing the immigrants' stories with moving photos and touching personal possessions, and clever visuals represent the country's ethnic diversity and immigration patterns. But the most evocative places are the vaulted Registry Room, restored to its 1920s state, and the medical examination rooms where 'weeding out' took place. Two per cent of applicants were deported – the Island of Hope was also called the Island of Tears. Such is the popularity of the ferry trip to Ellis Island (which also visits the Statue of Liberty – see **A-Z**) that the herding and queues will make you sympathize with the rigours of island visitors 100 years ago! The day's first ferry is the least crowded. See **SIGHTSEEING 1**.

Empire State Building: Completed in 1931 and 1454 ft high, this New York landmark, with its 73 elevators, 6500 windows and a beautiful marble lobby, was the tallest building in the world until the nearby World Trade Center (see **A-Z**) opened in the 1970s. The building is illuminated in different colours on public holidays (red, white and blue on 4 July, red and green at Christmas, and green on St. Patrick's Day – see **Events**). There are wonderful panoramas from the two observation platforms. King Kong's famous visit here with Fay Ray in the 1933 film is well recorded on the souvenirs for sale. In the concourse is the Guinness World Records Hall (see **A-Z**). The building is open until 2400 every day. See **SIGHTSEEING 2**.

Flatiron Building

Equitable Building: It was the building of this massive structure at No. 120 Broadway in 1915 that forced the city authorities to restrict the floor space of tall buildings and led to the multitiered style of architecture exemplified by the Rockefeller Center (see **A-Z**).

Federal Hall National Memorial: 15 Pine St/26 Wall St. This Parthenon-like building is on the spot where Washington took his oath of office as the first President of the US. Now a museum and national monument, it has also been a customs house and a bank. 0900-1700 Mon.-Fri.; Free. See **WALK 4**.

Flatiron Building: See **SIGHTSEEING 2**.

Ford Foundation Building: 320 E 42nd St, between 1st Ave and 2nd Ave. This building contains the first of New York City's indoor atriums, a semitropical garden set out between the L-shaped office blocks. See **WALK 3**.

Fraunces Tavern: 54 Pearl St. Samuel Fraunces was an innkeeper who became steward to President Washington. He owned this tavern, at the corner of Pearl St, where Washington took leave of his officers at the end of the War of American Independence. New York's oldest restaurant serves great breakfasts, as well as housing a museum that documents New York during the war (1000-1645 Mon.-Fri., 1200-1600 Sat.; Inexpensive). See **WALK 4**.

Frick Collection: The perfect museum to visit if you don't have much time to spare. The collection was established by Henry Clay Frick in 1914 and includes works by Van Dyck, Fragonard, Turner, Rembrandt, Whistler, El Greco and Gainsborough, as well as Vermeer's *Officer and Laughing Girl*. The museum is filled with 18thC furnishings and has a peaceful enclosed marble courtyard. There are free daily introductory talks and slide shows. See **MUSEUMS 1**.

Gracie Mansion: This mansion, on East End Ave at 88th St in Carl Schurz Park (see **PARKS**), was built in 1799 by the Scottish merchant

Grand Central Station

Alexander Gracie as his country home. It is now the residence of the mayor of New York. Tours by appointment only.

Grand Central Station: E 42nd St at Park Ave. The huge clock above the station entrance commemorates the railroad's founder, Cornelius Vanderbilt (see **A-Z**). The Grand Concourse itself is immense and there is a night sky with star constellations painted on the ceiling. An acoustic phenomenon just outside the Oyster Bar (see **RESTAURANTS 2**) allows you to whisper in one corner and be heard at the other end of the wide space. Free tours of this fine Beaux Arts building of 1913 are organized by the Municipal Art Society and leave from the Chemical Bank Concourse at 1230 on Wed. See **WALK 3**.

Grant's Tomb: The marble sepulchre of Ulysses S. Grant, Lincoln's supreme commander in the Civil War and President of the US between 1868 and 1876, stands on Riverside Drive at W 122nd St in Harlem (see **A-Z**).

Greenwich Village: What was once New York City's bohemia still has some of that atmosphere. Its shady streets and plethora of cafés and boutiques make it ideal for meandering strolls. While the brownstone houses are now prestigious addresses, still all humanity congregates in the streets, from coiffeured ladies exercising their dogs and students lugging cellos to winos who have passed out on a street bench. MacDougal St and Bleecker St offer a concentration of the best cafés and restaurants. See **CITY DISTRICTS**, **WALK 2**.

Guggenheim Museum: This amazing Frank Lloyd Wright building, completed in 1959 shortly after his death, resembles an upside-down beehive, or a giant snail, or a corkscrew. It has recently been much extended. Take the elevator to the top and work down. The upper floors have challenging exhibitions, while the lower floors have a superlative, dense collection of the greats of modern art: Picasso, Gauguin, Van Gogh, Klee, Kandinsky. A new branch of the Guggenheim, exhibiting largely works from the main museum, has opened in a renovated cast-iron building (see **A-Z**) at 575 Broadway at Prince St. See **MUSEUMS 1**.

Guinness World Records Hall: This little museum dedicated to the longest, shortest, highest, smallest, fattest, oldest, youngest and strangest achievements of mankind was set up in the concourse of the Empire State Building (see **A-Z**) when it was still the tallest building in the world.

Hamilton Grange: The home of Alexander Hamilton (c.1757-1804), first US Secretary of the Treasury (featured on $10 bills), is situated in Hamilton Terrace on Convent Ave at 142nd St, Harlem. Hamilton was killed in a duel by Aaron Burr who lived in the Morris-Jumel Mansion (see **A-Z**) and is buried in Trinity Church (see **A-Z**).

Harlem: This area, extending from 110th St to the Harlem River, had its heyday in the Jazz Age of the 1920s and '30s when the Cotton Club was *the* place to be seen. There are several attractions worth visiting, including Audubon Terrace (see **A-Z**), home to several museums; Cloisters (see **A-Z**); the Harlem River Houses at 151st St; Strivers' Row on 138th St between 8th Ave and Powell Boulevard, one of the finest terraces in New York; the Schomberg Center for research into black culture at Lenox Ave and 135th St; the Abyssinian Baptist Church; Grant's Tomb (see **A-Z**); Hamilton Grange (see **A-Z**); and the Morris-Jumel Mansion (see **A-Z**). The Studio Museum at 144 W 125th St has a fine collection of Afro-American art. For children there is also Aunt Len's Doll and Toy Museum at 6 Hamilton Terrace at 141st St (by appointment only, tel: 2814143). It is not always safe to walk in some parts of the area. Consider taking a tour (see **A-Z**). See **CITY DISTRICTS**.

Hayden Planetarium: The planetarium belongs to the American Museum of Natural History (see **A-Z**) and is mainly intended for the instruction and enjoyment of children. There are laser shows on Fri. and Sat. nights. See **CHILDREN**.

Helmsley Palace Hotel: 457 Madison Ave. Owned by the property developer Harry Helmsley, who also owns several other hotels which bear his name, the Helmsley Palace is famous for the clever incorporation of the beautiful 19thC Villard Houses, whose splendidly lavish interiors now form the hotel's public rooms. These mansions, based on the Cancelleria Palace in Venice, were originally built for the railroad owner Henry Villard.

Hudson River: The river flows along Manhattan's western side and divides New York City from Jersey City, and New York State from the State of New Jersey. The George Washington Bridge crosses the river from 178th St in Manhattan to Fort Lee in New Jersey. Two toll tunnels run under the river: the Holland Tunnel at Canal St and Hudson St, and the Lincoln Tunnel on 42nd St east of the Port Authority Bus Terminal.

Intrepid Sea-Air-Space Museum: See **WALK 3**.

Johnson, Philip (b. 1906): The grand old man of US architecture who designed the Seagram Building (see **A-Z**), along with Mies Van der

Rohe; the New York State Theater (see MUSIC VENUES); the AT&T Building (1984); the Citicorp Center (see **A-Z**); and the extensions to the Museum of Modern Art (see **A-Z**).

La Guardia, Henry F. (1882-1947): The New York City mayor who, from 1934 to 1946, cleaned up the city's administration after decades of corruption and scandal. One of New York's airports is named after him.

Lincoln Center for the Performing Arts: See MUSIC VENUES.

'Little Church Around the Corner': Properly called the Church of the Transfiguration, the church earned its title in 1870 when the pastor of a church refused to perform a funeral service for an actor and suggested 'the little church around the corner' instead. See CHURCHES.

Little Italy: The main attractions of this shrinking district are its shops and restaurants frequented by well-to-do New Yorkers but still redolent of both Mafia films and a European atmosphere. The main thoroughfare is Mulberry St, and the liveliest time of the year to visit is during the Feast of San Gennaio, a week of festivities in Sep. See CITY DISTRICTS.

Long Island: The island is 125 miles long but only 23 miles across at its widest point. The villages along the northern shore overlook harbours and beaches, and the cliffs are dotted with mansions built in the 1920s. Long, busy, sandy beaches stretch along the south shore. Long Island is the site of the quintessential suburban American development, Levittown. You can reach the island by train from Penn Station (see **Railways**) or by bus from the Port Authority Bus Terminal (see **Buses**).

Madison Square: The original home of Madison Square Garden (see **A-Z**), and the former centre of New York's theatre district, lies at the junction of 5th Ave and Broadway at 23rd St. The New York Life Building now occupies the spot where the theatre stood, and the Flatiron Building (see SIGHTSEEING 2) dominates the south side of the square.

Madison Square Garden: As its name suggests, Madison Square Garden was originally sited, in 1928, in Madison Square (see **A-Z**). This theatre, designed by Stanford White, has moved twice since and is now at 32nd St above Penn Station. In its heyday it was notorious as a place of scandal and debauchery. See **MUSIC VENUES**.

Marble Collegiate Church: This Gothic-style church, with its marble exterior, belongs to the longest-established Protestant congregation in the USA, founded in 1628 by the Dutch West India Company. Peter Minuit, Governor of New Amsterdam, was the first church elder, and Norman Vincent Peale, famous author of *The Power of Positive Thinking*, was pastor here for over 50 years. See **CHURCHES**.

Metropolitan Museum

Metropolitan Museum of Art: This huge, constantly evolving museum possesses some 2 million works of art, of which only 20% can be displayed at any one time. Needless to say, you shouldn't try to see everything or even all the main galleries in one visit. Highlights include the Temple of Dendur in the Egyptian collection; the exhibition of pre-Columbian gold in the Art of Africa, Oceania and the Americas; and the American Wing, spread over three floors, the most comprehensive collection of furniture, decorative arts and fine arts in existence. One of the world's greatest collections of European paintings has been newly displayed in an expanded space, allowing more of its renowned collection of Impressionists to be shown. If it all gets too much, take a breather in the Chinese Garden Court of the Ming Dynasty, or in the roof sculpture garden overlooking Central Park. There's also a café and restaurant. Ask about free conducted tours and tape tours of the main attractions, as well as of specific areas.

Note that if you're visiting Tue.-Thu., because of funding cuts some galleries are closed (tel: 5703711 in advance if you want to see something specific). At weekends the museum can be offputtingly busy. See MUSEUMS 1, WALK 1.

Midtown: This huge area between 14th St and 59th St takes in New York's Theater District (see CITY DISTRICTS), including Broadway (see **A-Z**); the prestigious shops along 5th Ave; most of the city's hotels; great landmarks such as as the Chrysler Building (see **A-Z**) and the Citicorp Center (see **A-Z**); many major museums; the Port Authority Bus Terminal; and Penn and Grand Central (see **A-Z**) stations. See **Orientation**.

Morris-Jumel Mansion: This mansion, on Edgecombe Ave at W 160th St in Harlem, was built as the country house of Roger Morris in 1765 and is decorated and furnished in the style of the period. Aaron Burr, the tempestuous Federal-period politician who killed Alexander Hamilton (see **Hamilton Grange**) in a duel, lived here during his retirement from politics. There are tours of the house, and its gardens are pleasant for picnics.

Museum of Modern Art (MOMA): Established in 1929, this permanent collection of painting, sculpture, design, drawing, photography and film traces the development of modern art from 1880. Enjoy the outdoor Sculpture Garden at ground level which contains statues by Henry Moore, Matisse and Rodin, as well as Picasso's *She-Goat*. Among the outstanding Impressionist and Postimpressionist works on the first floor are Van Gogh's *Starry Night* and Rousseau's *Sleeping Gypsy*. There are separate rooms for Monet's *Water Lilies*, Cubist paintings (some by Picasso and Braque) and works by Matisse. More modern American and abstract paintings and sculptures occupy the second floor, including works by Stella, Wyeth, Hopper, Warhol, and the New York school artists, Pollock, De Kooning and Rothko. On the third floor the emphasis is on architecture and design, with models of modern buildings, examples of Tiffany glasswork and Art Nouveau furniture. There are also galleries devoted to one of the most interesting collections of photographs in the world. Two theatres regularly show films, and there is a gift shop and the Garden Café (overlooking the Sculpture Garden). See MUSEUMS 1.

New York Botanical Garden: An indoor and outdoor 250 acre paradise, just north of the Bronx Zoo (see **A-Z**), containing rose, herb, rock and native plant gardens (open daily; Free). Travel to the garden by Metro-North from Grand Central Station.

New York Stock Exchange

New York Historical Society: Nineteenth-century American paintings (especially the landscapes of the Hudson River school artists), watercolours by the ornithologist James Audubon and lamps by Louis Tiffany are just some of the attractions in this collection housed on five floors. The museum also contains a reference library of works on American history, maps and prints tracing the development of the city from Colonial times, and displays of horse-drawn carriages. See MUSEUMS 3.

New York Public Library: You cannot miss this building, on 5th Ave between 41st St and 42nd St, fronted as it is by two large stone lions representing Patience and Fortitude. It was designed by Carrère and Hastings and opened in 1911. The library runs an excellent reference service and you can see some of the most splendid public rooms in the city on one of the popular conducted tours (1100 and 1400 Tue.-Sat.). See WALK 3.

New York Stock Exchange: 20 Broad St. The home of the 'junk bond' and the 'big bang' stands on the corner of Wall St and Broad St. The present building was opened in 1903, though dealing in stocks and shares has been going on around Wall St since the 1790s. You can view the Great Hall – the floor where the financial dealings are carried out – from the visitors gallery, while the visitor center provides up-to-date information on the workings of the exchange. See **WALK 4**.

Olmstead, Frederick Law (1822-1903): The architect who, along with his partner Calvert Vaux, won the competition to design Central Park (see **A-Z**). He planned it as a rural paradise, with the Utopian dream of bringing the countryside into the lives of the people of Manhattan. Vaux and Olmstead also designed Riverside Park (see **PARKS**), Morningside Park and Prospect Park (see **A-Z**).

Olympic Tower: 645 5th Ave. The black glass exterior of this apartment block built in 1976 reflects St. Patrick's Cathedral (see **A-Z**) which stands nearby. It has one of the many public atriums in New York City.

Pan Am Building: 200 Park Ave, between E 44th St and E 45th St. With the demise of the airline, the building has been bought and renamed by Metlife. It was designed by, among others, Walter Gropius, who modelled the tall, black structure on the shape of an aeroplane wing, and opened in 1963. It towers over Grand Central Station (see **A-Z**) and shuts off Park Ave to the south.

Pierpont Morgan Library: The prominent banker J.P. Morgan (1837-1913) had this building built in 1902 to hold his massive collection of medieval manuscripts, Renaissance books and works of art. His son, J.P. Jnr, gifted the library and building to the public in 1924. The best pieces from the collection are displayed in the original library. See **MUSEUMS 2**.

Plaza Hotel: W 59th St at 5th Ave. The hotel was built in 1907 and is named after Grand Army Plaza at the southwest corner of Central Park (see **A-Z**), and is one of New York City's most popular hotels. The famous Oak Bar offers refuge from the bustle of 5th Ave.

Queens: This is the largest borough in New York City. The Astoria area is a good place to sample Greek cuisine, while Jackson Heights is the spot to find South American food. Jamaica Bay is a bird-watcher's paradise (there are some 300 bird species to be seen), and the Rockaways, which encloses the bay, is a 10 mile stretch of beach.

Riverside Church: Climb the 400 ft tower of this Gothic Revival-style church, inspired by the cathedral at Chartres in France and financed by John D. Rockefeller Jnr (see **A-Z**), for one of the most impressive views of the city skyline. It was built in 1930 and inside are figures by Jacob Epstein. The world's largest carillon (74 bells) gives recitals on Sat. and hols. See **CHURCHES**.

Rockefeller Plaza

Rockefeller Center: The main building at the heart of this complex, stretching from 48th St to 52nd St and 5th Ave to 7th Ave, is the GE Building (see **SIGHTSEEING 2**), formerly the RCA Building, the home of NBC Studios and the famous Rainbow Room Restaurant. The plaza in front of the GE Building is an ice-skating rink in winter and an outdoor dining area in summer (note the huge statue of Prometheus with his torch). At Christmas time a large tree is erected in front of the GE Building, the Channel Gardens are extravagantly decorated with angels, and the restaurants and shops throng with Christmas shoppers. One of the complex's finest structures is the Radio City Music Hall (see MUSIC VENUES), a national landmark building with a splendid interior described as being 'Art Deco's true shrine'– so splendid, in fact, that the murals from the men's toilets are now in the Museum of Modern Art (see **A-Z**)! There are interesting backstage tours, tel: 6324041. See SIGHTSEEING 1, **Rockefellers**.

Rockefellers: One of New York's, and America's, wealthiest and most powerful families. The family fortune was amassed by John D. Rockefeller (1839-1937) who established Standard Oil (Esso) as the leading oil company. His son, John D. Rockefeller Jnr, put his father's multimillions to good use, assisting in the financing of the Riverside Church (see **A-Z**) and agreeing to build a new opera house for the Metropolitan Opera. The latter ended up, with the help of John D. Rockefeller III, in the Lincoln Center (see **A-Z**). Nelson A. Rockefeller was Governor of New York State from 1958 to 1974, and vice-president from 1974 to 1976.

Roosevelt Island: Known as Blackwell Island before 1921, after the family who farmed the island and lived in the clapboard farmhouse on Main St (open to the public) from 1796 to 1804, it became known as 'Welfare Island' when the city administration established a prison, hospital, poorhouse and lunatic asylum here. Now it is a pleasant residential area. You can reach it by aerial tramway from 60th St and 2nd Ave.

St. Bartholomew's Church: This large, ornate, Byzantine church of 1919 by Bertram Goodhue stands at Park Ave and 51st St. The Sun. afternoon concerts held here in autumn and winter are justly famous. There are also concerts at 1200 on Wed.

St. John the Divine: Construction began in 1892 on this huge Gothic-style cathedral, but one-third of the building is still unfinished. You can watch the masons at work cutting and carving stones using medieval methods, visit the Biblical Garden, or attend one of the regular concerts held here. See CHURCHES.

St. Mark's in the Bowery: Peter Stuyvesant (c.1610-72) was the last Dutch Governor of New Amsterdam and this church was built in 1799 on the site of the chapel on his farm or *bouwerie*. He is buried under the cobbled yard. The church was damaged by fire in 1979 and is undergoing restoration. See **CHURCHES**.

St. Patrick's Cathedral: This famous Gothic-style cathedral was designed by James Renwick and seats 2500 people. The main body of the building was completed in 1878, with the towers being added between 1885 and 1888. The white marble and stone exterior is over 300 ft high and is studded with intensely blue stained-glass windows. Walk round to the back to visit the Lady Chapel and the crypt, which houses the remains of former cardinals. Look out for the red ceremonial cardinals' caps suspended from the ceiling in the sanctuary. See **CHURCHES**.

St. Paul's Chapel: The oldest church (1766) in Manhattan resembles St. Martin-in-the-Fields in Trafalgar Square, London. This was George Washington's place of worship and his pew can be seen in the north aisle. Original Waterford crystal chandeliers light the beautiful Georgian interior. Classical music concerts are held here. See **CHURCHES, WALK 4**.

St. Peter's: See **CHURCHES, Citicorp Center**.

St. Thomas' Church: This slightly lopsided Gothic-style church on 5th Ave at W 53rd St has interesting carvings over its doors. There is, for example, a $ sign entwined with the lovers' knot above the Bride's

Door! You can hear choral music here at 1200 on Wed. and organ recitals on Sun afternoon.

Seagram Building: This deceptively simple building, the first in the Modernist style when built in the 1950s, has been widely copied. Its architects, Philip Johnson (see **A-Z**) and Mies Van der Rohe, paid close attention to detail. The original glass and bronze metal exterior has now weathered to grey. A huge theatre backcloth by Picasso decorates the famous Four Seasons Restaurant. See **SIGHTSEEING 2**.

SoHo: The name of this area is short for *So*uth of *Ho*uston (pronounced 'Howstin') and is synonymous in New York City with art galleries. It was once inhabited by the trendy crowd who moved here from Greenwich Village (see **A-Z**). They were displaced by the monied set who gradually followed them here, driving them onto the district of TriBeCa (see **A-Z**). The enduring thing about SoHo is its cast-iron buildings (see **A-Z**). Those in Greene St are excellent examples but you should also look out for the Haughwout Building at Broome St and Broadway, and the Little Singer Building on Prince St and Broadway. See **CITY DISTRICTS**.

Statue of Liberty

South Street Seaport: To describe this regenerated area as New York's equivalent of London's Covent Garden, with hosts of buskers and outdoor dining, does not do justice to the beauty of the setting. Views of Brooklyn Bridge (see **A-Z**) and cruisers and speedboats vie for attention with the glass-fronted Downtown skyscrapers seen through the rigging of old clippers. The centre of this area, on the eastern tip of Manhattan, is occupied by Piers 15-18, where several sailing ships are moored. You can also take a 3 hr cruise round the harbour in summer on the schooner *Pioneer*. One of the district's liveliest spots is the Fulton Fish Market which must be visited extremely early (about 0500). A good introduction to the district is provided by The Seaport Experience which regularly screens a film tracing the area's history from the 19thC. Schermerhorn Row contains some of the oldest buildings in New York, including warehouses, and two seafood restaurants called Sweet's and Sloppy Louie's, which re-create the service, but not the prices, provided to traders and sailors in the past. There is also a large number of interesting shops selling items relating to the trades and crafts of the Seaport's heyday. See **SIGHTSEEING 1**, **WALK 4**.

Staten Island: This once-rural borough became suburbanized with the opening of the Verrazano Narrows Bridge (see **A-Z**) in 1964. However, you can still visit Staten Island the old-fashioned way on the ferry (see **SIGHTSEEING 1**, **Ferries**). Bus M113 will take you from the dingy terminal to the two most interesting sites on the island: the Jacques Marchais Center for Tibetan Art, 338 Lighthouse Ave, Richmond, and the Richmondstown Restoration, 441 Clark Ave, Richmondstown. The former houses a remarkably complete collection of bronzes, paintings and musical instruments inside Buddhist temple buildings. The latter is an 18thC working village where you can watch the skills and techniques of the period being demonstrated. There is also a Children's Museum and a zoo which has a notable collection of rare rattlesnakes.

Statue of Liberty: Every year 3.5 million visitors head out to *Liberty Enlightening the World* (the full name of Frederic Auguste Bartholdi's statue) on the Circle Line Ferry (see **Ferries**), so expect long

Empire State Building

queues (you should allow about 4 hr for the visit). The enormous statue of Liberty, the interior iron framework of which was engineered by Gustave Eiffel, was restored for her 100th birthday in 1986. A museum containing displays on the restoration, as well as on immigration, is located in the base, which is emblazoned with Emma Lazarus' poem *New Colossus*, the most famous lines of which are: 'Give me your tired, your poor/Your huddled masses yearning to breathe free'. Tel: 5633200 for information. See **SIGHTSEEING 1**.

Temple Emanu-El: America's largest synagogue and New York City's leading Reform synagogue is on 5th Ave at 65th St. The synagogue was built in 1929 and features a superb wheel window, and a Byzantine-influenced chapel with twin domes. 1000-1700.

Times Square: Originally called Longacre Sq., the area was renamed after the old building at No. 1 Times Sq., which is the former home of *The New York Times*. Although the square is slightly seedy, it has a magical quality at night, with all the billboards, theatre queues and neon lights. Besides being at the centre of New York's Theater District (see **CITY DISTRICTS**), it is also the place New Yorkers come to celebrate New Year. See **SIGHTSEEING 1**, **WALK 3**, **Broadway**.

TriBeCa: The name is short for *Tri*angle *Be*low *Ca*nal (St). Twenty years ago small textile firms lined the district's streets. Now the warehouses have been converted into residential pads for artists (who emigrated from SoHo – see **A-Z** – when it was yuppified), celebrities and generally the better off. As in SoHo, there are many superb cast-iron buildings (see **A-Z**), and a concentration of them can be found on White St. See **CITY DISTRICTS**.

Trinity Church: This Episcopal church built in 1846 in Gothic Revival style on Broadway at Wall St is dwarfed by the twin towers of the World Trade Center (see **A-Z**). It houses the graves of Robert Fulton, the inventor of the steamboat, and Alexander Hamilton (see **Hamilton Grange**), first Secretary of the Treasury. Concerts are held on Tue. See **CHURCHES**, **WALK 4**.

Trump Tower: This huge block was designed in 1983 and contains 230 apartments, all of which have views on three sides. It is named after the developer Donald Trump, who lives here along with many other multimillionaires. Galeries Lafayette (see **SHOPPING 2**) is situated in the building's six-storey atrium of shops and restaurants. See **SIGHTSEEING 2**.

Tudor City: Composed of a group of 12 (supposedly Tudor-style) buildings ranging from ten to 32 storeys in height, Tudor City surrounds a little park at the east end of 42nd St behind the United Nations (see **A-Z**). Its turrets are best seen from the East River (see **A-Z**) as you cruise past on a Circle Line Ferry (see **Ferries**).

United Nations: The Secretariat Building is the most easily identifiable as it is the tallest of the United Nations headquarters complex. The low-lying domed building is the General Assembly where members of the public can attend General Assembly meetings (free tickets are available on a first-come, first-served basis, distributed just before 1030 and 1530). Other attractions include the gardens, Chagall's stained-glass windows, and the delegates' dining room. See **SIGHTSEEING 1**, **WALK 3**.

Uptown: Anywhere north of 59th St is Uptown. In directions, it can refer to anywhere north of where you are at present. See **Orientation**.

Vanderbilts: Together with the Astors (see **A-Z**) and the Rockefellers (see **A-Z**), the Vanderbilts are one of the three most famous families in New York. Their fortune was amassed by the infamous 'Commodore' Cornelius (his rank came from running the Staten Island Ferry – see SIGHTSEEING 1) who ruthlessly exploited the development of steamships and railroads. His son William inherited $100 million from him in 1877, and doubled that sum within eight years. Gertrude Vanderbilt Whitney, the Commodore's granddaughter, was an excellent sculptor and a patron of the arts. Her collection forms the basis of the Whitney Museum of American Art (see **A-Z**). Gloria Vanderbilt is a well-known fashion designer.

Verrazano Narrows Bridge: At 4260 ft, this is the world's longest suspension bridge. Built in 1964, it links Brooklyn (see **A-Z**) to Staten Island (see **A-Z**) over the stretch of water named after the explorer Giovanni di Verrazano, who first sighted the estuary of the Hudson River (see **A-Z**) in 1524.

Villard Houses: See **Helmsley Palace Hotel**.

Waldorf-Astoria: This is possibly the best-known hotel in New York. The site, at 301 Park Ave between 49th St and 50th St, is the hotel's second home. Originally two hotels, the Waldorf and the Astoria, stood at 34th St, where the Empire State Building (see **A-Z**) now is.

Wall Street: See WALK 4, **New York Stock Exchange**.

Washington Square: The area now occupied by Washington Square, at the heart of Greenwich Village (See **A-Z**), was once a duck marsh, then a paupers' cemetery, and finally a parade ground, before town houses were built on it in 1836 and solid members of society took up residence. The architectural style of the period is preserved only on the north side of the square which is now the centre of New York University. Stanford White's Triumphal Arch, originally made of wood, was erected in 1889 to commemorate the centenary of Washington's inauguration. It was replaced by a stone arch in 1892. Statues of Washington, both in and out of uniform, adorn the north side of the arch. Garibaldi, the great Italian soldier and politician, is also memorialized in stone. See PARKS, WALK 2.

Whitney Museum of American Art: The museum, founded by Gertrude Vanderbilt Whitney (see **Vanderbilts**) in 1930 and installed in its present building designed by Marcel Breuer in 1966, houses wonderfully provocative exhibitions of 20thC American art, such as Calder's mobiles and stabiles. The permanent collection includes the Abstract Expressionists: high priests Pollock and De Kooning, Reinhard's *Black Painting*, Warhol's *Coke Bottles* and John's *Three Flags*. A branch of the main museum at Philip Morris, 42nd St and Park Ave, features a sculpture court, changing exhibitions and a café. See MUSEUMS 1.

Woolworth Building: 233 Broadway. Facing City Hall Park across Broadway, the Woolworth Building, built in 1913, is one of the most popular buildings in New York. Designed for Frank W. Woolworth (of the famous chain of shops), it celebrates his commercial success in a Gothic style he chose after visiting Europe. F. W. paid $13.5 million in cash for the building and a series of humorous caricatures in the lobby depicts the owner, the architect (Cass Gilbert) and the builders exchanging the building for money. See WALK 4.

World Trade Center: Built between 1966 and 1977, the twin 110-storey towers of the World Trade Center dominate the skyline of Manhattan. Over 50,000 people work here. The main attractions are the two observation areas in No. 2 World Trade Center, the south tower, which offer breathtaking views of the city, especially just before dusk when Manhattan gradually changes into a giant kaleidoscope of lights. At the top of No. 1 World Trade Center is the famous Windows on the World Restaurant which is very expensive, but serves excellent food and has the best wine list in America. In 1974 Philippe Petit performed for one hour on a tightrope which had been strung between the towers. See SIGHTSEEING 2.

TRUMP TOWER

Accidents & Breakdowns: In the event of an accident follow the usual procedure of exchanging names, addresses and insurance details. To contact the police or other emergency services, tel: 911. If someone is injured and you are held responsible, insist on contacting your embassy or consulate (see **A-Z**) as soon as possible. In the case of breakdowns contact the American Automobile Association (AAA) at Broadway and 62nd St, which offers an emergency road service to members, tel: 212-7573356, or phone the nearest garage. Tel: 212-7572000 for a report on road conditions before you set out. See **Driving**.

Accommodation: There are 100,000 hotel rooms in more than 1000 hotels in New York City, which range in price from $40 in a no-frills YMCA to $325 in the luxurious Waldorf Towers. You should expect to pay the following in the various categories:

De Luxe	over $250	Budget	$70-100
Luxury	$150-250	Basic	under $70
Moderate	$100-150		

In addition, there is a 6% tax on hotel rooms under $100, 11% tax on rooms over $100, plus a sales tax of 8.25% and a bed tax of $2 per person. It is advisable to make hotel reservations in advance of visiting the city, especially in spring and autumn when the hotels are filled with convention delegates. If you do arrive without a reservation Meegan Hotel Reservation Service at JFK International Airport (see **Airports**) provides a booking service for a wide range of hotels, tel: 718-9959292. Although the New York Convention and Visitors Bureau (see **Tourist Information**) does not provide this service, it can issue you with a list of hotels with their price ranges and telephone numbers (0900-1800 Mon.-Fri., 1000-1800 Sat. & Sun.). The following types of accommodation are also recommended:

Women only – Martha Washington, 30 E 30th St, tel: 212-6891900; Allerton House, 130 E 57th St, tel: 212-7538841. Both basic and cheap.

Manhattan East Suite Hotels – Tel: 1-800-6378433 or 212-9717010 for locations and prices. Suites with kitchenettes for the price of most luxury hotel rooms.

Bed and Breakfast – Urban Ventures, 306 W 38th St, tel: 212-5945650; City Lights Bed and Breakfast, 308 E 79th St, tel: 212-7377049; New World Bed and Breakfast, 150 5th Ave, tel: 212-6755600. Book in advance. A two-night minimum stay may be required. Prices range from $60 to $90. See **Camping & Caravanning**, **Youth Hostels**.

Airports: New York City is served by three major airports: John F. Kennedy International Airport (JFK) – 15 miles from Midtown Manhattan in southeast Queens. Handles international flights. Transport to and from the airport includes the Carey Bus (see **Buses**) which departs every 30 min for Grand Central Station and the Port Authority Bus Terminal in Midtown Manhattan (1 hr; $11), and a free shuttle bus connecting all the airline terminals to the subway system (only recommended if you have few items of luggage and are travelling during the day). Take Train A marked Far Rockaway to Howard Beach Station at JFK (1 hr 30 min). Taxis (see **A-Z**) are the easiest form of transport to

and from all the airports (approximately $35 from JFK).
Newark International Airport (EWR) – 16 miles from Midtown Manhattan in northeast New Jersey. Handles international flights. Olympia Trail and NJ (New Jersey) Transit provide bus transport into Manhattan (40 min; $7). The taxi fare is $40.
La Guardia (LGA) – 8 miles from Midtown Manhattan in northwest Queens. Handles internal flights. Connections to Manhattan include the Carey Bus to Grand Central Station and the Port Authority Bus Terminal (30 min; $8.50), and the Delta water-shuttle service (tel: 1-800-2211212 for a timetable) from Pier 11 at the end of Wall St or 34th St Pier to Marine Air Terminal (approximately 30 min; $15). The taxi fare is $20.
There are no tourist offices at the airports (see **Tourist Information**). Tel: 800-AIRRIDE for further information on transport to and from the airports.

Art Galleries: In addition to all the public galleries in New York City, there are 400 private galleries along Madison Ave (in the high 60s and 70s) and 57th St, plus those in SoHo (see **A-Z**) and the East Village (see **A-Z**). See MUSEUMS 1-3, **Museums**.

Baby-sitters: Contact the Baby-sitters Guild, 60 E 42nd St, tel: 6820227, or the Baby-sitters Association, 610 Cathedral Parkway, tel: 8659348, for a list of more agencies or for guidance. Hotel receptions also have lists of baby-sitters. See CHILDREN, **Children**.

Banks: See **Currency**, **Money**, **Opening Times**.

Best Buys: Things to look out for are fashions, jewellery, linens, china, records and tapes. Keep an eye out for sales where you can pick up goods at discount prices. New York is also the most price-competitive city in the US for camera, video and electronic equipment. See SHOPPING 1-3, **Markets**, **Shopping**.

Bicycle Hire: It is possible to hire bicycles in Central Park (see **A-Z**) at the Loeb Boathouse. In Manhattan you can also hire them at Pedal Pusher, 1306 2nd Ave, between 68th St and 69th St; Midtown Bicycles, 360 W 47th St at 9th Ave; and Sixth Avenue Bicycles, 546 6th Ave at 15th St. However, riding a bicycle in the city can be dangerous. If you must hire one you will have to produce ID. The cost is approximately $6-8 per hr, and a deposit is required. Consult the *Yellow Pages* for more hiring outlets.

Budget: 1993 prices.

Nightclubs	$20 admission, $5 per drink
Broadway show	$30-60
Off-Broadway show	$15-35
Cinemas	$7.50
Museums	$2-7 (some ask for donations; many are free on Tue. evening)
Breakfast	$5 (local coffee shop), $10 (hotel)
Lunch	$6 (sandwich and drink)

Buses: City buses (MTA) have blue numbers (preceded by the letter M) and display a list of streets through which they pass (in red). They require an exact fare of $1.25 in coins or tokens (purchased from subway token booths). Place your fare in the box at the front of the bus upon entering and if taking an intersecting route ask for a free transfer (if you are not sure, ask the driver). There are no tourist or weekly passes. The service runs 24 hr, but is less frequent late at night. The buses are clean, punctual and comfortable, but slow. The city's main bus station, the Port Authority Bus Terminal, at 40th St and 8th Ave, has three tiers of shops, eateries, and bus platforms with connections to destinations all over the US. You can also catch the NJ Transit buses to Newark Airport and the Carey buses to JFK and La Guardia airports at the Airport Bus Center. Many weirdos, drug addicts and winos hang about this area so carry your own baggage and hail your own taxi. You can reach the terminal on subways A, C and E or buses M10, M11, M16, M27 and M42.

Cameras & Photography: Films, batteries and VHS (NTSC) tapes are sold in drugstores, electronics shops and some delis. Nikon House, 620 5th Ave and 50th St, has a free photo gallery and repair centre, holds seminars on photography, gives out free information on cameras, and rents out equipment, tel: 5863907. Always ask in museums and galleries to establish if photography is permitted. See SHOPPING 3.

Camping & Caravanning: There are no camp sites in New York City itself, but on Long Island (see **A-Z**) there are the Old Bethpage, at Claremont Road and East Islip, and the Heckscher State Park, tel: 516-7944222 (Long Island Convention and Visitors Bureau). Tel: 212-8276255 (New York State Convention and Visitors Bureau) for the state's travel guide with camping details.

Car Hire: Driving in New York City is most definitely not recommended. If you want to hire a car for touring outside the city you must be 25 years of age, and have a credit card and valid driving licence (foreign licences accepted). Collision damage waiver and personal injury insurance are advisable. The names and addresses of hire firms are listed in *Yellow Pages*. Look out for special weekend and weekly rates advertised in newspapers. The cost of hiring a car is approximately $50 per day. See **Driving**.

Chemists: Known as drugstores or pharmacies. Kaufman Pharmacy at 50th St and Lexington Ave is open 24 hr, tel: 7552266. See **Health**.

Children: In addition to the attractions listed in the topics section of this book (see **CHILDREN**), there are special children's activities available throughout the five boroughs which you can check for in the local press. *The New York Times* has a 'For Children' section on Fri., as does the weekly *New York* magazine. But if in doubt, head for the area of Central Park (see **A-Z**), stretching from 5th Ave and 59th St to 110th St, where there is a zoo, a carousel, a puppet theatre, rowing boats for hire, horse-riding and roller-skating. Favourite sightseeing trips include boat trips (see **Ferries**), and going up the Empire State Building (see **A-Z**) and World Trade Center (see **A-Z**). See **Baby-sitters**.

Cinemas: Some cinemas do not sell tickets for popular first-run films until 1 hr before they start. In addition to the usual mix of first-run, cult and golden oldie films shown in cinemas, there are special screenings by the Museum of Modern Art (see **A-Z**) and the Alliance Française, 22 E 60th St. See **What's On**.

Climate: Spring is usually mild, but can sometimes be unpredictable and rainy (average 10°C). Autumn is normally clear, sharp and short-lived (average 14°C). The winter months, from Nov. to Mar., are cold (average 4°C), while summer can be extremely hot and humid (average 23°C). Tel: 9761212 for recorded weather reports.

Consulates:
UK – 845 3rd Ave, tel: 7450200.
Republic of Ireland – 515 Madison Ave, tel: 3192555.
Australia – 636 5th Ave, tel: 2454000.
Canada – 1251 6th Ave, tel: 7682400.
New Zealand – No New York consular service, tel: 202-3284800.

Conversion Chart:

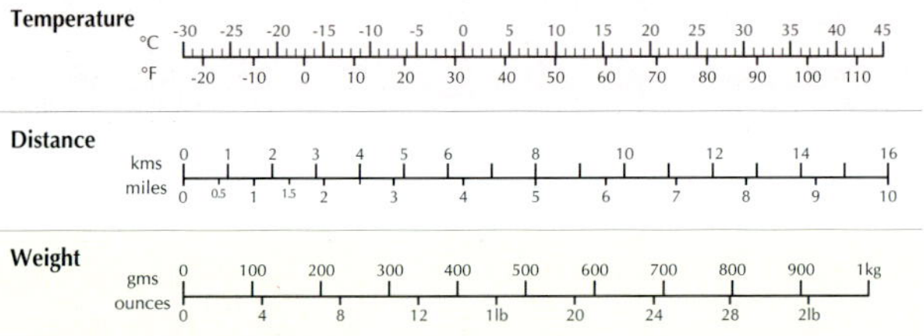

Credit Cards: See **Money**.

Crime & Theft: If you're used to big cities, New York may not seem unduly dangerous (statistically, many other US cities have worse crime levels). If you're not, then the best way to visit some areas, such as Harlem (see **A-Z**), is with a group (see **Tours**). A few tips: don't let anyone carry your baggage for you and always hail your own taxi. You should always try to avoid travelling on the subway (see **A-Z**) at night. Keep valuables in hotel safe-deposit boxes. If you are mugged, take a taxi to the nearest precinct (police station) and report the crime immediately (the police will refund the cost of the fare). The police (see **A-Z**) will record the theft and give you a reference number for your insurance company. If you have a credit card or traveller's cheques stolen, also contact the company which issued them as soon as possible (see **Money**). See **Consulates**, **Emergency Numbers**, **Insurance**.

Currency: The dollar ($) is the US monetary unit, divided into 100 cents (c).
Coins – 1c (penny), 5c (nickel), 10c (dime), 25c (quarter) and 50c (half a dollar).
Notes (bills) – $1, $5, $10, $20, $50 and $100.
Be careful what you hand over and receive, because all the notes are the same colour. See **Money**.

Customs Allowances:

Duty Free Into:	Cigarettes	or Cigars	or Tobacco	Spirits	Wine
USA	200	50	4.4 lb	1 *l*	1 *l*
UK	200	50	250 g	1 *l*	2 *l*

Disabled People: A general access guide to the city for people with disabilities is available from New York City's mayor's office at 52 Chambers St, NY, NY 10007, tel: 212-5660972. An access guide to the city's cultural institutions is available from Hospital Audiences, 220 W 42nd St, NY, NY 10036. Almost all buses but few subways can cater for those in wheelchairs. Tel: 718-5968585 for information. See **Health**.

Drinks: The water in NYC is perfectly safe to drink and there is no need to order bottled water unless you prefer it. The selection of alcoholic drinks available in the city is phenomenal – anything from a classic Manhattan cocktail (try one at the Stanhope opposite the Metropolitan Museum of Art – see **A-Z**) to beer brewed right in the heart of the city. The better restaurants all offer extensive selections of wine from America (New York State and California), France, Italy, Germany and Australia. There are short tours of New York City's only winery, Schapiro's at 126 Rivington St, on Sun. See **BARS**.

Driving: Consider hiring a car only to make an excursion from the city (see **Excursions**). Driving is not a good idea in New York City, with its vast network of roads and highways, and especially not in Manhattan. The headache of traffic jams, especially during rush hours (0800-1000, 1630-1800 Mon.-Fri.) and the expense of parking (see **A-Z**) can be avoided by using public transport (see **Transport**) and taxis (see **A-Z**). Drive on the right-hand side of the road. The speed limit in NYC is 35 mph but that speed is rarely reached. Seat belts are compulsory. If you are caught in an intersection when the light changes you are liable to be given a hefty fine by traffic police. Right turns through a red light are not permitted and pedestrians have the right of way at crossings. See **Accidents & Breakdowns**, **Parking**, **Petrol**.

Drugs: All drugs are illegal and there are severe penalties for offenders. Contact your embassy or consulate (see **A-Z**) if you are arrested for a drugs-related offence.

Eating Out: Make sure you experience a breakfast New York-style: eggs any way you want, or pancakes, or waffles. Don't miss out on the institution of Sun. brunch either. This can sometimes be an enormous buffet and is best enjoyed with the Sun. papers. Delicatessens, or delis, are a New York trademark. Often open 24 hr a day, their voluminous sandwiches make a filling lunch. The eye-catching fruit displays outside many delis have become one of the city's strongest images. As well as steaks and seafood, and some of the best New American (i.e. post-*nouvelle cuisine*) restaurants around, you can eat whatever ethnic food you want in New York: Italian everywhere (*not* at its best in Little Italy), Chinese in Chinatown, French (look for bistros in Greenwich Village), and Indian on E 6th St between 1st Ave and 2nd Ave and in Little India (Lexington Ave from E 27th St to 29th St), not to mention Japanese sushi bars, and, for the adventurous, Polish, Russian and Korean cuisine. If all that sounds a bit exotic, there's always a McDonald's or Pizza Hut nearby. Zagat's is the best restaurant guide to the city (available in bookshops). Tel: 777-FOOD for information on well-rated restaurants and delivery services. See RESTAURANTS 1-3, **Food**.

Electricity: 110-115 V. Small two-pin plugs are used. Adaptors are available in New York and at airports. Establish before leaving whether your appliances will need a voltage transformer (although travel appliances often have a dual-voltage switch).

Emergency Numbers:

Police, Fire, Ambulance	911
Crime Victims Hotline	5777777
Missing Persons	7199000
Police Information	3745000

Events:

January: New Year's Eve celebrations in Times Square; Boat Show; Chinese New Year.
February: Dog Show.
March: Cat Show; *17:* St. Patrick's Day Parade.
Easter Sun.: Easter Parade.
April: Baseball season starts (see **Sports**).
May: Ninth Avenue International Festival.
May-June: Washington Square Outdoor Art Show.
June: Feast of St. Anthony; Metropolitan Opera Concerts in Central Park; Gay Pride Day Parade; Jazz Festival.
July: Summer pier concerts at South Street Seaport; Summer Garden at Museum of Modern Art; Shakespeare Festival in Central Park; *4:* Harbor Festival.
August: Lincoln Center Out of Doors Festival; Harlem Week.
August-September: Washington Square Outdoor Art Show.
September: US Open Tennis Championships (see **Sports**); Feast of San Gennaio; New York is Book Country; Steuben Day Parade.
October: Columbus Day Parade; Hallowe'en Day Parade.

November: NYC Marathon; Thanksgiving Day Parade.
December: Christmas tree at the Rockefeller Center.
Check the local press for details of the hundreds of ethnic and neighbourhood festivals held throughout the year (see **What's On**).

Excursions: One- or two-day excursions to the following destinations are recommended: Atlantic City, Saratoga, Lake George in upstate New York, Fire Island/Montauk and Long Island (see **A-Z**). American Express Travel Agency has nine branches in the city, including those at 65 Broadway, tel: 4936500, 374 Park Ave near 51st St, tel: 4218240, 199 Water Seaport Plaza, tel: 9436947, and one in Bloomingdale's (see **SHOPPING 1**), tel: 7053171. See **Tours**.

Ferries: The Circle Line Ferry, tel: 5633200, will take you around Manhattan on a 3.5 hr cruise from Pier 83 at the end of W 42nd St. Circle Line ferries also leave from Castle Clinton in Battery Park (see **PARKS**, **A-Z**) for Liberty Island and the Statue of Liberty (see **A-Z**), tel: 2695755 for information. Seaport Line, tel: 1-800-5522626, has a 90 min cruise around the tip of Manhattan leaving from Pier 16 at South St. The Staten Island Ferry (see **SIGHTSEEING 1**) which leaves from Battery Park is good value at 50c.

Staten Island Ferry

Food: New York has a vast range of restaurants from every culture imaginable. Just on the streets you have the choice of anything from hot dogs to pretzels, pizzas to ice creams, sodas to souvlakia, and kebabs to honey-roasted nuts! See **RESTAURANTS 1-3**, **Eating Out**.

Health: Standards of medical care in New York are high, but treatment is very expensive. It is therefore essential to take out adequate insurance (see **A-Z**) before leaving home. City hospitals are as follows:
Bellevue Hospital, 1st Ave at 27th St, tel: 5614141.
Manhattan Eye, Ear and Throat Hospital, 210 E 64th St, tel: 8389200.
New York University Medical Center, 550 1st Ave at 23rd St, tel: 2637300.
Columbia Presbyterian Medical Center, 662 W 168th St, tel: 3052500.
Lenox Hill Hospital, Park Ave at 77th St, tel: 4392345.
Mount Sinai, 5th Ave at 100th St, tel: 2416500. See **Chemists**.

Insurance: You should take out adequate travel insurance covering you against theft and loss of property and money as well as medical expenses. Your travel agent should be able to recommend a suitable policy. See **Car Hire**, **Crime & Theft**, **Health**.

Laundries: Self-service Laundromats charge $1.25 per load of washing and $1 per load of drying. Laundry rates in hotels are listed. Dry-cleaning costs $6-7 per suit and $2-3 per shirt.

Lost Property: For articles lost on a bus or on the subway, contact the New York City Transit Authority Lost Property Unit, tel: 718-6256200. For articles lost in taxis, tel: 221-TAXI.

Markets:
Food – Stalls between 111th St and 116th St on Park Ave in Spanish Harlem specialize in Mediterranean foods; a covered market in Essex St in the Lower East Side offers a wide range of foodstuffs; there are also green markets run by the city which sell local farm produce at various locations in town, such as at the World Trade Center and Union Sq.
Clothes – On Sun. stalls selling clothes appear in Orchard St in the Lower East Side; the SoHo Emporium at 375 W Broadway contains dozens of stalls selling unusual hand-crafted clothing and jewellery at reasonable prices.
Collectables – The Annex Antiques Fair and Flea Market at 26th St and 6th Ave offers nostalgia items, antiques and curiosities (Sun.); the

outdoor Canal Street Flea Market at 335 Canal St is good for antiques and jewellery (weekends Mar.-Nov.); another flea market on Columbus Ave, between 76th St and 77th St, deals in a wide range of goods – books, records, film posters, jewellery, clothes, etc. See **Shopping**.

Money: You can change currency and traveller's cheques at banks and bureaux de change, although many banks will only cash cheques for their own customers. Check beforehand if they charge a fee or commission (some don't) and what these are likely to be. Bank Leumi Trust Company of New York, 579 5th Ave, and Deak New York Inc., 630 5th Ave, both specialize in exchange services, and many of the offices of international banks, such as Citibank and Chemical Bank, will change currency at standard rates. All the major credit cards (American Express, Mastercharge/Access, Visa, Diners Club, Carte Blanche) are readily accepted in hotels, restaurants and shops, and by car hire firms. If you lose a credit card call the relevant office immediately (American Express cardholders should tel: 1-800-5282121). American Express, Visa and Thomas Cook traveller's cheques in US dollars are accepted by banks, hotels, most shops and restaurants. Identification is required. See **Currency**, **Opening Times**.

Museums: New York City has museums to suit every taste and interest. In addition to those listed in MUSEUMS 1-3 in the topics section, and described in the cultural/historical gazetteer, the following are recommended: the Numismatic Society in Audubon Terrace (see **A-Z**); Japan House, 333 E 47th St; and the Library and Museum of the Performing Arts in the Lincoln Center (see **A-Z**) at 111 Amsterdam Ave. See **Art Galleries**.

Newspapers: Daily newspapers include *The New York Times*, an American institution and a traditional armful of reading, which offers the best international coverage; the *New York Post*, containing local news and scandal; the *Daily News*, New York's 'hometown' paper, with good local news coverage and gossip; *New York Newsday*, mostly appealing to Queens and Long Island suburbanites; and the business-orientated *Wall Street Journal*. See **What's On**.

Nightlife: When do New Yorkers sleep? Greenwich Village at 2400 on a Fri. night is as busy as Wall St on a Mon. morning. One of the joys of New York is being able to drink and party into the small hours of the morning. Whatever you fancy doing you can – it's just as easy to spend the evening at an outrageous gay club as listen to a classical concert. Though admission charges are often very affordable, drinks can be extremely expensive and there may be a two-drink minimum. Discos may enforce a dress code (try to look trendy and/or show lots of flesh!). If you like just being part of a happening evening scene, head downtown to Greenwich Village (see **A-Z**), the East Village (see **A-Z**), TriBeCa (see **A-Z**) and SoHo (see **A-Z**). Midtown is not safe at night, so have a specific destination in mind. See **BARS**, **MUSIC VENUES**, **NIGHTLIFE 1-4**, **Cinemas**, **Theatre**, **What's On**.

Opening Times:
Bars – 0800/0900 (1200 at latest)-0400 Mon.-Sat. (until 0300 Sun.), although some close earlier.
Shops – 0900/1000-1800 Mon.-Sat. (until 2100 Thu.), some 1200-1800 Sun. In Downtown districts clothes shops are open until 2000, while boutiques in nightlife areas close very late.
Banks – 0900-1500 Mon.-Fri. Some also Sat. am. There are also 24 hr automatic teller machines.
Post Offices – 0800-1700 Mon.-Fri., 0800-1200 Sat.

Orientation: New York is an easy city to find your way around. This is especially true of the area of Manhattan north of 14th St, which is laid out on a grid system of avenues, which run north-south, and streets, which run east-west. Fifth Ave divides the east side from the west side of town. Uptown (see **A-Z**) is north of 59th St, Downtown (see **A-Z**) is to the south of 14th St, and Midtown (see **A-Z**) is in between. The numbering of buildings east or west starts at 5th Ave (1 E 8th St is just east of 5th Ave, and 1 W 8th St is just west of 5th Ave). Equip yourself with a detailed street map as well as bus and subway maps from the visitor bureau (see **Tourist Information**). If you are walking anywhere it will take at least 15 min to cover ten blocks going north or south. Those running east and west take longer.

Parking: Read signs carefully before parking, as it is expensive to reclaim a car that has been towed away. Car parks are very expensive, typically up to $15 per hr at Park Ave and $10 per hr Downtown, though they are proportionately less expensive for a whole day. Expect to pay for hotel car parking too. See **Driving**.

Passports & Customs: A valid passport is necessary, but no visa is required for stays not exceeding 90 days, and provided you have a return ticket. If you intend leaving the USA and re-entering, you should enquire about a visa at the US embassy in London, tel: 071-4996846. See **Customs Allowances**.

Petrol: Known as gas in the US. Many garages are open 24 hr. Unleaded petrol is available everywhere. Expect to pay around $1.20 per gallon in the city for self-service, but more for attended service. See **Driving**.

Police: In Downtown Manhattan there is a high police presence on foot, on horseback, on motorcycle and in distinctive blue and white cars. Regular police wear blue uniforms with a precinct label in a patch on their left arm. The number of transit police has increased considerably over the last few years. Traffic police wear a brown uniform. See **Crime & Theft**, **Emergency Numbers**.

Post Offices: The main post office at 33rd St and 8th Ave is open 24 hr, seven days a week. The other major Midtown post office is at 45th St and Lexington Ave. It costs 40c to send a postcard to the UK and 50c for a letter (1993 prices). See **Opening Times**.

Public Holidays: 1 Jan.; 3rd Mon. in Jan. (Martin Luther King Day); 3rd Mon. in Feb. (President's Day); last Mon. in May (Memorial Day); 4 July (Independence Day); 1st Mon in Sep. (Labor Day); 2nd Mon. in Oct. (Columbus Day); 11 Nov. (Veterans Day); last Thu. in Nov. (Thanksgiving Day); 25 Dec. Most shops are closed on New Year's Day, Thanksgiving Day and Christmas Day. At other holidays shops stay open for special sales and bars are open until 0400.

Railways: Train services to upstate New York, Boston and New England depart from Grand Central Station on 42nd St at Park Ave, tel: 5324900. The station's meeting point and round information booth are both situated in the main hall beside the clock. There are underground connections from here to other buildings. Amtrak trains to Washington DC, the Long Island Railroad and the New Jersey Transit all leave from Penn Station at 33rd St and 7th Ave. Trains are generally clean and punctual. For Amtrak (the US railroad company) information, tel: 1-800-USARAIL.

Religious Services: Every possible religious affiliation is represented in New York. Call the following numbers for information: Roman Catholic, 3711000; Episcopalian, 3167400; Islamic, 5335060; Jewish, 7532288; Lutheran, 5326350; Presbyterian, 8702101. Consult the Manhattan *Yellow Pages* for the addresses and telephone numbers of many more churches and temples.

Shopping: New York City is a showcase for the world's merchandise. You'll find branches of all the famous retail chains here as well as every kind of speciality shop imaginable. The best shopping and browsing areas are SoHo (see **A-Z**) and the Lower East Side, Manhattan's bargain basement, 5th Ave (34th St to 59th St), Madison Ave (59th St to 72nd St) and Columbus Ave (72nd St to 86th St). There are antique shops in the

east 50s and 80s along Madison Ave in SoHo, but those in Brooklyn (see **A-Z**) along Atlantic Ave, between Hoyt St and 3rd St, are generally cheaper. A city sales tax of 8.25% is levied on every purchase. See SHOPPING 1-3, **Best Buys**, **Markets**, **Opening Times**.

Smoking: New city-wide laws prohibit smoking in public places such as theatres, lobbies, office buildings, etc. There is no smoking in elevators, in subways or on trains and buses. Restaurants must provide both smoking and nonsmoking areas.

Sports:
Spectator Sports:
American Football – Meadowlands Stadium (Aug.-Dec.), East Rutherford, NJ. Tel: 201-9358500 for tickets for the New York Jets games and 201-9358222 for tickets for the New York Giants.
Ice Hockey – Madison Square Garden (Oct.-April). Tel: 465-MSGI for tickets for the New York Rangers.
Baseball – Shea Stadium in Queens, home of the New York Mets, tel: 718-5078499; Yankee Stadium in the Bronx, home of the New York Yankees, tel: 718-2936000.
Basketball – Madison Square Garden (Nov.-April). Tel: 465-MSGI for details of New York Knicks games.
Tennis – Flushing Meadow Park, Queens. Venue of the US Open Tennis Championships (Sep.). Tel: 718-2715100 for tickets. Subway 7 to Shea Stadium/Willets Point.
Horse Racing – Aqueduct Race Track in Ozone Park, Queens (Oct.-May), tel: 718-6414700; Belmont in Elmont on Long Island (May-Oct.), tel: 718-6414700. Harness racing (trotting) takes place in Yonkers; Roosevelt Raceway in Westbury, Long Island; Meadowlands, East Rutherford, New Jersey. Check times with the New York Racing Association, tel: 718-6414700.
Participatory sports:
Golf – Midtown Indoor Golf Club, 7 W 45th St (golf simulators), tel: 7191494.
Fishing – Hudson River off Manhattan along Riverside Park Esplanade from W 72nd St to 84th St, and from W 91st St to 100th St.

Swimming – Outdoor public pools (end May-beginning Sep.) at 59th St and West End Ave, and at the East River at 77th St. Also check with local YMCAs.
Tennis – There are more than 500 public tennis courts in New York. Tel: 8303133 for information on those in Manhattan.
Horse Riding – Claremont Riding Academy, 175 W 89th St, Central Park, tel: 7245100.
Ice-skating – Rockefeller Center Skating Rink (Oct.-April).
Roller-skating – Roller skates and skateboards can be hired from or bought at Blades West, 105 W 72nd St, tel: 7873911.

Subway: The subway operates 24 hr, seven days a week, and each day 3.5 million passengers are carried. The fare is a flat $1.25 and there are no concessions or weekly passes. You can purchase subway tokens at the booths in the stations (some also have vending machines). It makes sense to buy ten at once to avoid future queueing. Tokens can also be used on buses (see **A-Z**). The subway provides the fastest means of travelling long distances across town but stations offer few amenities apart from some telephones, benches and a few stores in the larger ones. Both the stations and the system have undergone refurbishment with the addition of new subway cars and the cleaning up of graffiti. In summer, though the stations can be stifling, air-conditioning makes the

trains pleasantly cool. Although the subway is relatively safe during rush hours, avoid travelling alone on it at night and wait for trains in the well-lit areas in front of the ticket booths. Trains are designated either by letter or number (depending on which company they originally belonged to). A good map of the subway is essential.

Taxis: Although there are 11,787 taxis in New York City, it is hard to find a cab during rush hours and in wet weather. Make sure the cab you hail is a licensed and metered yellow cab (identifiable by the medallion on top). The light on the roof indicates when the cab is for hire. The fare starts at $1.50 and accumulates at a rate of 25c per fifth of a mile and every 75 seconds waiting in traffic. There is a 50c surcharge between 2000 and 0600, and you will be expected to give a tip (see **Tipping**). The average taxi fare for a journey across town works out at around $5 (up to four people can share a cab for the same fare). Midtown to Uptown is approximately $6 and Midtown to Downtown is $5-10 (drivers do not like changing large bills). Not all drivers have a good knowledge of the city. Be as exact as possible about your destination and know how to get there. Take the computerized printout receipt you are given when you leave the taxi, as it has the number of the cab and phone numbers for lost property and complaints.

Telephones & Telegrams: There are plenty of coin-operated public telephones on street corners and in restaurants, hotels, bars, etc. Local calls cost 25c for the first 3 min and then 10c for each block of 3 min thereafter. The area code for Manhattan is 212, and that for the Bronx, Brooklyn, Queens and Staten Island 718. When dialling numbers in a different code area, precede the code with 1. Telephones have letters alongside the numbers on the dial or keys, and some services use letters instead of numbers, e.g. for a wake-up call tel: 5409253, which is also 540-WAKE. Hotels usually levy additional charges on phone calls. Check what these are before dialling, especially overseas. Telegrams (cables) can be sent by phone through Western Union on 1-800-3256000, or from post offices (see **A-Z**). There is also a public fax machine in the lobby of the Empire State Building (see **A-Z**). See **Emergency Numbers**.

Television & Radio: Check the daily newspapers (see **A-Z**) for complete television listings, including terrestrial, cable, HBO (Home Box Office), Cinemax, ESPN (all sports) and CNN (all news) channels. Free tickets for TV shows are available by writing or calling the network concerned. There is a huge choice of radio stations to choose from on both AM and FM, with everything from news to jazz and sport to 'urban contemporary' music.

Theatre: Although it can be expensive (see **Budget**), you should not leave New York without a visit to the theatre. Tel: 5632929 for recorded information about what is playing on Broadway and Off-Broadway. Theatre tickets can be purchased directly from the box office or by writing in advance. Call Telecharge on 2396200 or Ticketmaster on 3074100 to charge tickets by phone (there is a surcharge for this service). Ticket Central at 406 W 42nd St sells tickets for Off-Broadway shows and the TKTS ticket booth at the north end of Times Sq. sells discounted theatre tickets for performances both on and off Broadway. If you don't mind queueing and are willing to take a chance, you can get half-price tickets after 1500 for evening performances, and after 1000 on Wed., Sat. and Sun for matinees. There is another generally less busy TKTS booth at No. 2 World Trade Center (1100-1730 Mon.-Fri., 1100-1530 Sat.). The underused kiosk in Bryant Park specializes in music and dance tickets. A large selection of free 'twofer' vouchers is available at the New York Convention and Visitors Bureau (see **Tourist Information**), which gives about one-third off tickets for a selection of longer-running shows when you purchase tickets at the theatre box office. Shakespeare in the Park at the Delacorte Theater in Central Park makes a wonderful free evening's entertainment in the summer (Tue.-Sun., June-Sep.). Queue by the theatre for the free tickets that are distributed at 1800 – be there by 1400 to collect a coupon – for performances at 2000. See MUSIC VENUES, **What's On**.

Time Difference: New York is 5 hr behind GMT.

Tipping: In restaurants you should leave 15-20% of the total bill as a tip (New Yorkers usually just double the 8.25% tax). Taxi drivers expect

companies, with outlines of what each offers.
Bus tours – Gray Line, 254 W 54th St, tel: 3972620, offers the widest range of tours, including hop-on, hop-off trolley tours. Shortline, 166 W 46th St, tel: 3972620.
Scheduled helicopter flights – Island Helicopters on E 34th St, tel: 6834575; Liberty Helicopter Tours, W 30th St and 12th Ave, tel: 1-800-5429933. From around $40. These are very noisy, but very exhilarating, especially at night.
Walking tours – A Walk of the Town, tel: 2225343; Municipal Art Society, tel: 4391049; Talk-a-Walk (cassettes), tel: 6860356; Museum of the City of New York, tel: 5341672.
Harlem – Harlem Tours offers jazz, gospel and sightseeing tours. Harlem Spirituals, 1697 Broadway, Suite 203, tel: 7570425; Harlem Your Way! Tours Unlimited, 129 W 130th St, tel: 6901687.
Central Park Trolley Tours, three times per day, tel: 3973809; Urban Park Rangers Walks, tel: 4274040.
See **Excursions**, **Ferries**.

Transport: Walking is the best means of seeing New York. The subway (see **A-Z**) is fast and therefore best for longer distances, but not

a 20% tip, and porters and bellhops should be given around $1 per item of luggage.

Toilets: These can be found in public buildings such as museums, stations, shopping centres, etc. Those in bars and restaurants can also be used, although some have a 'patrons only' sign.

Tourist Information: You can get up-to-date information on events, programmes, shops and restaurants throughout the city, as well as obtain free bus, subway and tour maps, 'twofer' coupons (see **Theatre**) and sightseeing brochures at the New York Convention and Visitors Bureau. Although they can also advise on accommodation, they do not make hotel bookings. The offices are at 2 Columbus Circle, tel: 212-3978222 (0900-1800 Mon.-Fri., 1000-1800 Sat., Sun. & hols).

Tours: The New York Convention and Visitors Bureau (see **Tourist Information**) publishes comprehensive details of sightseeing and tour

This book was produced using QuarkXPress™ and Adobe Illustrator 3.2™ on Apple Macintosh™ computers and output to separated film on a Linotronic™ 300 Imagesetter

Text: Paul Gunnion,
with additional information by Fred Mawer
Photography: Doug Corrance
Electronic Cartography: Susan Harvey Design and Iain Robinson (1)

First published 1990 Second Edition 1994

Published by HarperCollins Publishers
Printed in Italy by Amadeus S.p.A.
ISBN 0 00 470501-7

The publishers welcome corrections and suggestions from readers; write to: The Publishing Manager, Travel Guides, HarperCollins Publishers, PO Box, Glasgow G4 0NB.

always very pleasant. Taxis (see **A-Z**) are plentiful and can be an adventure. See **Airports**, **Buses**, **Ferries**, **Railways**.

Traveller's Cheques: See **Money**.

What's On: The weekly *New York* magazine lists restaurants, museums, theatre and cinema programmes, music and dance venues, sales and bargains. The weekly *New Yorker* magazine combines listings with sophisticated and entertaining reviews. The official *City Guide* is a free weekly journal of highlights, sightseeing attractions, Broadway shows, etc. which is distributed to hotels. The weekly (Wed.) *Village Voice* is an exhaustive trawl of New York City's entertainments, both mainstream and offbeat. *The New York Times* has a special arts and leisure section on Fri. and Sun. See **Events**, **Newspapers**.

Youth Hostels: No special youth or student ID is required. Book well in advance. New York International Youth Hostel, 891 Amsterdam Ave at W 103rd St, tel: 212-9322300 (shared rooms); Vanderbilt YMCA, 224 E 47th St, tel: 212-7552410; Sloane House YMCA, 356 W 34th St, tel: 212-7605850; West Side YMCA, 5 W 63rd St, tel: 212-7871301. All the YMCAs listed have private rooms and charge around $40 per night.